A BIAS OF REFLECTIONS

A BIAS OF

REFLECTIONS

Confessions of an Incipient Old Jew

NATHAN PERLMUTTER

Arlington House   New Rochelle, N.Y.

Dedicated to Ruthie,
my wife and my friend.

Acknowledgments

I am deeply indebted to my wife, Ruthann Perlmutter, for her firm editorial guidance throughout the creation of this book. She it was who when I was careless of authenticity, inattentive to style, watched over them. So much so that hopefully they may be recognized here and there, in the pages that follow. Failing their frequent recognition, the reader might justifiably admonish me that I should have heeded her more often.

I wish also to express my appreciation to *Midstream, National Review, National Jewish Monthly,* and *Congress Bi-Weekly* for their permission to reprint those essays which they had originally published.

Contents

Prologue

The ensuing pages are commentary about being Jewish, about being middle aged, about the liberal political tradition in which my generation grew up.

To be Jewish, at least in a gentile world, is to be somewhat neurotic, and so the commentary slips here and reveals chauvinism, slips there and shows its self-doubts. Being Jewish is also a state of mind conditioned by gentiles. That's why in Israel Jews are Israelis and in the Diaspora we are Jews. This being the case, how could I write about myself without writing about Them? So I write about Them, the white gentiles and the black gentiles.

And I write about these, my middle years, a good time for pausing. The long rear view is still well lit, and I can see clearly the way by which I came. And in my late forties the distance is long enough ahead for me to care about it, and in these pages I do that. It's occurred to me— Shall I say, "Admittedly"?—that middle age might well be a neurosis too, conditioned by its own gentiles, the Young.

And the commentary is opinionated on matters political. How could a Diaspora Jew's diary be otherwise? Strong political views, whether fears or biases, whether illusions or delusions, have been propellants, for us, driving us inwards from the margins of America, driving us outwards from our own marginality. And make no mistake, in our time and in this place, it's been the politics of the Left that has opened and freshened the way. There on the Left is where America's windows have been raised.

But now the times seem foreign and all of our remembered places are changing, and of late, I am beginning to feel a draft from the windows through which yesterday breezes wafted. I write about that too.

GROWING UP WITH GOD, JEWS, AND GENTILES

Before I begin what I want to say, I want to say something.

As far back as I can remember, I seem to have always known that I was Jewish. Likely it all began with my parents telling me I was, and they seeming fairly reliable it never occurred to me to question them. Besides, in Williamsburg everybody who was anybody was Jewish. (The Williamsburg in Brooklyn, that is.) They looked like me, they dressed like me, they spoke like me. Plainly then, I too must be Jewish. So I grew up Jewish.

This means that I became a gentile watcher, although it was sometime before I realized there were more of Them than of Us. It means too that as I grew older, sailed the BMT and our trolley car lines out of Williamsburg, beyond Brownsville, penetrating the exotic gentile lands in the Brooklyn bush, I developed several mild neuroses common to growing Jews. For instance, resenting my being different long before resenting Them for their intolerance of my differences. And, of course, in New York, in the 1930's, growing up Jewish wasn't at all inconsonant with growing older secular. Sometimes I have even thought being Jewish is a stage which agnostics have outgrown.

So, fittingly, we begin at the beginning. My child self with and without God, a boyhood's field guide to gentiles, and name changing as social camouflage, all of it viewed from an elevation of years, and with a bias of reflections.

Who Screwed Who

*I declare for agnosticism. They must've
screwed. Surviving God. I take Him
back. An old and stooped, thousand
wrinkled Jew. A pitching pennies losing
streak. For the first time in my life, I
pray. The 1930's as lean God years. I am
a decompression chamber.*

When at age eleven, I conceded to myself that I was unable to figure out "who made God," no matter I had
thought about it so hard it dizzied me, I consulted *Funk
and Wagnalls.* I carried them to the long table in the library's reference room and riffled the pages to "agnostic"
and then to "atheist." The seen spelling of the exotic
words was a kind of theological decolletage, a delectation
savored, but nervously, like reading porno in a public
place. In those furtive moments, I declared for agnosticism.

My doubts about God's origins arose because Bernie,
one of the "big guys" (he had already been *Bar Mitzvah*),
wanted me to play handball with him, and I was begging
off, lest I be late for Hebrew School.

"So what if you're late? C'mon, play."

"I can't."

"Why? What's so important?"

"I gotta go. If I don't, I'll get a sin."

17

Bernie looked surprised, probably feigned. "A sin? You must be kidding! Who's going to give it to you? Who, for instance?"

"God! You a jerk or something? God!"

I thought that I had scored, perhaps decisively, but I wasn't sure. It had been too easy. He must have known *that*.

"Where'd you come from?" He was being conversational, addressing me like a teacher, leading you to your own answers.

"What d'you mean, where'd I come from? South Third Street. You know that."

"No, no, no. Who made you? You know, how'd you get born?"

"My mother and father."

"And how'd they make you?"

"Aw, come on! You know. They must've screwed."

"Right. And who made them?"

I wanted out—the conversation suddenly seemed claustrophobic—but I was locked into it, my answers being pulled from me by the strings of his questions. "Their mothers and fathers screwed too," and feinting aggression, "What'd you think?"

"Right. And who made them? Your great grandparents! Right?"

"Yeah, sure."

"Now go all the way back. Go back a trillion years. Adam and Eve made the first people. Right? Right. And God made Adam and Eve. Right? Right. But who made God? *WHO SCREWED WHO TO MAKE GOD?* Who? Huh? Who?"

Nightly, for weeks on end, I thought so hard about Bernie's question, my scalp tingled and my hands formed involuntary fists as if clenched they would somehow propel my struggling brain to the Secret of God. But always my slowly, methodically reviewed string of begats were dead-ended at Who Made God. In time however, tortuous though the enigma was, I found that I was surviving it. God, however, was not doing as well, and finally in the library, opting for agnosticism, I suspended my judgment of Him.

It was when I was thirteen, on the very morning, in fact, of my *Bar Mitzvah,* and right there in the synagogue, that God returned for me and I was so grateful to Him, I took Him back.

It happened because we had a pushcart vendor in our neighborhood, an old and stooped, thousand wrinkled Jew, who sold *knishes. Knishes* so delicious, a man could steal just to taste one. And I did. Actually I didn't quite steal them. What several of us used to do was to buy them on trust. They cost three cents a *knish,* but who could eat only one *knish*? And who had six cents? So we bought one for cash and the second on trust. At the end of a week, it wasn't unusual to be fifteen, even twenty one cents in debt to him. On the morning of my *Bar Mitzvah,* I was *two* weeks in arrears with virtually no prospects of settling up. (I was deep in a pitching pennies losing streak.) Guilt-ridden, I had been avoiding his street corner, while letting word get to him that I had a serious case of double pneumonia.

This then was the ethical murkiness in which my morning of mornings dawned. Services in our small synagogue were well along, and as anticipated there was the rabbi's signal to me to rise, come front and center and read from the bible, become *Bar Mitzvah,* perform the very rites of manhood. I rose, my knees more shaken than my spirituality, moved to the lecterned bible, looked out upon the two dozen elderly morning worshippers and there in their midst, his Ancient Mariner's eye impaling me on the Ark of the Covenant, was the *knishes* man!

I prayed. Oh, how I prayed. For the first time in my life, I *really* prayed. I prayed to God to placate the *knishes* man, or failing that, to scatter his memory, or to restrain him from rising from his bench and accusingly point his gnarled and crooked finger at me, or to strike him dumb so that his wrath would be unheard and unsensed by all of the suddenly frightening old men whose staring eyes like prickly quills surrounded me. And during the intensive while my brain feverishly prayed my defense, my boy's innocent alto sing-songed the morning's portion of the bible. And then, in minutes only, it was over. The *knishes* man had neither risen, or *j'accused* me. Instead, God had made him doze off.

My faith peaked that morning. Several months later, however, I had had it with God. I was in the "rapid advance" class of the eighth grade, a special class for gifted children. The semester was divided into three grading periods. It was necessary to pass the first of these periods in order to remain in the class and thereby graduate a year sooner than the time normally required. Illness having kept me out of class for several weeks, my marks ranged from plodders' D's to F's. It very much looked like I was going to be dropped back into the regular eighth grade. Still feeling God's grace (had I not paid the *knishes* man in full?), I again called on Him. I reminded Him of my illness, explained its effect on my grades, assured Him that given another chance I could easily catch up, and solemnly promised everlasting good behavior, and even daily prayer. All that I asked, not really for me, God, for my mother, was another chance.

I didn't get it. I flunked out. That night I decided that if there was a God, and He could be so small about something so big, then I wanted no part of him.

Those were bad times for God and me. Not only was I questioning His existence and when granting it for the sake of argument, faulting His pettiness, but I was growing aware of new and troubled conversations engaged in by my elders. Uncles playing gin rummy at my *Tanta* Ida's, their wives hand-cupping glasses of tea, seated 'round the kitchen table, neighbors idling on the stoop or in front of the candy store, were increasingly talking of a modern day Haman, a terrible anti-Semite in Germany, and not a one of them, not even quietly wise Mr. Zeitz who taught *Talmud Torah*, could explain why God, if there was a God, didn't stop the Nazis from hurting and shaming us. These were my early teens, and the rational foundation of Bernie's Who Screwed Who, the injustice of my personal illness, the malevolence or indifference, it didn't matter which, of a Supreme Being toward Germany's Jews all combined to make the 1930's lean God years.

My agnosticism, or more accurately, my indifference to questions of a Supreme Being, has grown old with me. I am simply incapable of entertaining faith in that which cannot be rationally explained. Curiously, however, as I have grown older I have grown more and more Jewish minded, Jewish feeling. Curiously, because this feeling is an expression not of the rationalism that supports my agnosticism, but of a romantic mysticism which while it nourishes my identification as a Jew, I cannot tap for generating faith in God or in religion. And it's this rational rejection of God and my romantic marriage with the Jewish people that now in my middle years, in my fatherhood of grown children, has come home to roost.

Sociologists have estimated that thirty percent of my generation's college attending children are marrying non-Jews. This while synagogues in America, *sans* our

children, *sans* us, increasingly resemble senior citizens'
enclaves. My generation seems to have served as a decompression chamber, entered into by our parents as Jews
without doubts, exited from by our children as doubtful
Jews. What's happened I think is that the rationalism
with which we pried ourselves free of our fathers' to us
irrelevant religious Judaism, now our children's inheritance and in their service, is prying them loose from our to
them irrelevant romantic Jewishness.

George Washington's Descendants

When all the world was Jewish. George Washington's Polish descendants. Wintertimes, when it snowed. The Italians as kin folk. Emerson and Thoreau. The Board of Directors of Consolidated Edison. I'm at it again.

When I was a boy in Williamsburg, our neighborhood was virtually all Jewish, and our neighborhood being our world, I assumed that the world was all Jewish, or just about. To be sure, we were aware that there were Christians, President Hoover for instance, and in American History George Washington (we suspected that Lincoln was one of us), and we knew that there were many Christians, mostly hard drinking and Jew tormenting, in "the old country," far beyond the ocean's horizon at Coney Island. I said, "or just about." I mean that we did have Christians in our neighborhood, and they seemed to be distributed one family to a tenement house and they all being janitors, I assumed that all Christians were janitors, and the Stanleys and Annas of them all being Polish, Christians, it followed, were Polish janitors. I sometimes wondered at the fallen state of George Washington's descendants.

As I grew older, eight, nine, and began walking long walks to other neighborhoods, I discovered the Irish and the Italians. The south side of Williamsburg was Jewish,

the north side, Italian. It was with the Italians that we
had our fights. Winter-times, when it snowed, we'd pile
high arsenals of snow balls, some filled with coal ashes,
some with horse dung, and our gangs would engage each
other across the no man's land of Metropolitan Avenue.
But we never really considered the Italians as full blooded
Christians, or as enemies. Perhaps because it was the Pole
who figured in our parents' accounts of old world anti-
Semitism, perhaps too because the Italians were neither
blond, nor thin lipped, but whatever, the Italians, albeit
antagonists, were a kind of distant kin.

I'm not quite sure just when, but it was late in my
young manhood, that I became aware of Protestants as
contemporary Christians, as distinguished from history
book-Germanic sects wakening to the rousings of Martin
Luther. Somehow I sensed them to be more civilized, less
anti-Jewish than Catholics. Theretofore I had considered
Christians as being pretty much all the same, and if dif-
fering amongst themselves, inconsequentially, like the
physiological differences between a Thai and a Cambodi-
an. Soon, I "liked Protestants better than Catholics."
Protestants were suggestive of England and in my Brooklyn neighborhood that meant "cultured." They were
Emerson and Thoreau, Brahmins, graced in Letters and
with a social conscience, yet; they were Jefferson and both
Roosevelts, providing an imagined patrician sanction for
my vague stirrings of made-in-Europe democratic-social-
ism. Viewed thusly, I classified Protestants alongside the
Italians of my earlier youth as not being fully Christian,
like the Catholics were, the "real" Christians, who
taunted us or whose fathers haunted our memories.

Even today, the word Catholic registers in me images
of Irishmen and of eastern and southern European nation-
ality groups, their ism coming on later, with thought. And

for all that I know better, the word Protestant conjures icons of socially haloed patricians, a kind of group photograph of the board of directors of the Bell Telephone Company or of Consolidated Edison, to be followed, but only upon reflection, by the garden variety Protestant sects.

Today, however, I suspect my Protestant icons, and find myself disposed more kindly to my ethnic images of Catholics.

I've thought about both changes in me and in the case of Catholics it has a lot to do with the ethnicity of the Catholic, the Irishness, or Italianness of him that is his resonancy, and which is proving more durable than his crucified, bleeding-Christ-statuary, my boyhood's nervously heard ticking time bomb in all Christians. Also, John XXIII figures in the change, and no matter that Lincoln turned out to be not really Jewish, I'm at it again, this time suspecting that John was, at least on his mother's side.

As to those Protestant icons, it figured that I would have a change of heart. How long can one, and a Jewish one at that, remain innocent about Con Ed?

Nathans: Hale, Bedford Forrest, Perlmutter

Being a Nathan was sometimes trying. Becoming Nathaniel Perl-mutere. They accommodate and I trim. There are ways and there are ways of secreting the yellow star.

I used to envy my brother his name, and recall once accusing my mother of having favored him, else why did she name me Nathan and him Philip, tell me that, ma, tell me that.

He had King Philip and if day-dreaming that association wasn't pleasure enough, there was the then movie star, Phillips Holmes. All I had was Nathan Hale. Admittedly, Nathan Hale would have been fine—except that among our schoolyard ditties was the couplet:

> *Nathan Hale,*
> *Nathan Hale,*
> *He shit in a pail,*
> *Shit in a pail.*

Being a Nathan was sometimes trying.

In those days, my surname, Perlmutter, never bothered me. Why should it have? In a family of Finkelsteins, Mandelmans, and Hubermans, in a neon milky way of

27

Gluckstern and Moscowitz and Lupowitz signs, Perlmutter rang euphonically true—not a Cabot or a Lodge, but a serviceable, respectable name. It was when I had graduated high school and, job hunting, charted my days by the help-wanted classified ads in the *New York Times,* that Perlmutter began to pinch.

Column after page long column, each packed tight with employment agency advertisements, stipulated "Chr only." "Chr" I quickly gathered meant Christian, not in code, but in the economics of per line ad rates. At eighteen I was sufficiently experienced to know that after several days of fringing scarves, I had "had it" with factory work, so these were "office job" ads I was handicapping. What eighteen years had not taught me however was that Perlmutter was a dead giveaway that I wasn't a Chr. Upon learning that one's name could be like one's color, a tribal badge, I experimented with pronouncing my name as Perl-mutere, hoping that this imagined Frenchifying of Perlmutter would permit me to pass. It didn't. I went further. In an interview with one of the Wall Street employment agencies, I not only gave them the Perl-mutere bit, but introduced myself as Nathaniel Perl-mutere. (I suppose it could be said of me that I was changing my Christian name.)

Over the years I've grown accustomed to Nathan. (It was some years after I had gotten over Nathan Hale's plumbing problems that I learned of General Nathan Bedford Forrest. He founded the Ku Klux Klan, but I never brought it up to my mother.) Perlmutter too sits well with me now, and I think it's because being comfortably Jewish in a gentile world, while being of both worlds, takes aging, time in which They accommodate for Perlmutter, time in which Perlmutter trims to the Diaspora, and all the contemporaneous while, time in which one grows accustomed to oneself, *qua* Jew, *qua* American, *qua* person.

Of course it's more than name changing that I mean to talk of. Being Jewish pinched then when anti-Semitism was manifest, and apparently it still has hair-shirt qualities for some young, no matter the change in the *Times*.

I'm not aware of any statistics on the subject, but I suspect that fewer young Jews contemplate changing their names today than did in my youth. But there are ways and there are ways of changing one's name, of secreting one's yellow star, no matter it is of the mind, not the sleeve, self conjured, rather than Made By Anti-Semitics. Becoming a universalist, for instance. Being so preoccupied (but publically and declaratively) with the social condition of other-than-Jews, indeed of anti-Jews, Black Panthers for instance, or Arab guerrillas, so that you make evident to all, yourself included, that though you were born Nathan Perlmutter, the real you, the you that is freer and bigger than your parochial-sized Jewish ancestors, is Nathaniel Perl-mutere.

The man at the employment agency on Wall Street sniffed the Nathan of me and I didn't get the office boy's job. What is saddening about the universalists is not that today's style of name changers aren't any smarter than we were, but that they have yet to learn that anti-Semites haven't changed much either.

GROWING OLDER WITH JEWS AND GENTILES

Before I begin what I want to say, I want to say something. Young people, *Parents' Religion: Jewish,* is what several of the following reminiscences are about. No matter I camouflage my middle age in recollections of my eleven year old self, I am aware that the incipient Old Jew of me shows through and nowhere as clearly as when I discuss today's Jewish young. And if here and there my philosophizing about them seems tolerant, I confess that I have worked at it. I am trying to age gracefully. If at other times I am crotchety, I'm afraid it came easily.

But if young Jews are the mirror in which I have watched myself grow older Jewisher, I have noted it elsewhere too. In my intolerance of intolerance for instance, and so I beat up an older man whom I would have reasoned with or ignored, when I was young; in my deepening sense of community with those Jewish exotics who live west of the Hudson River; in my responses, man and boy, to Israel.

I Beat Up an Old Man

I beat up an older man. It's a Yiddish store.
The next thing I knew. "Stop him!" Were
the candy store people really not Jewish?
A satisfied and peaceful frame of mind.

Several years ago I beat up an older man. I was in my early forties, he in his mid-fifties.

It was a Sunday, about 7:30 in the morning, in the Yorkville section of Manhattan and I was going for a *Times*. Our news dealer was closed, so I continued walking. On the next block, the man, who in minutes I would be pummeling, was coming toward me, carrying the *Sunday Times*.

"Where'd you get the paper?"

He stopped despite it being very cold: "You go down two blocks, and on the corner . . ." etc.

I thanked him, he said you're welcome, and he repeated the directions. I remember thinking, "polite man." He had a thick German accent. He jay-walked across the street and I continued, but in a moment I saw an open candy store across the street. It sold papers and I started toward it.

Now it began happening. The man, who had already crossed the street, turned and as our eyes met, I felt prompted to explain why I wasn't following his patiently given directions. "This place is open," pointing to the candy store. His raised-voice answer was, or incredulously I thought it was, "Don't go in there. It's Yiddish. Jews own it."

In real life, at least in mine, tense moments have not been distinguished by inspired prose. What I said was, "What was that?" and heart pounding, I changed course to walk toward him. "It's a Yiddish store. Jews own it. Stinking Jews. Don't go in there." Facial expressions italicized his intonated hatred.

Early Sunday morning in Manhattan is always unreal. But this! My own neighborhood, albeit German Yorkville, a loud Jew hater replete with German accent and me, whose career had been spent in the employ of the Anti-Defamation League and the American Jewish Committee. My shock ebbed quickly—as quickly hate rose in me. "You sonofabitch. I'm Jewish damn you, and if you weren't older than me, I'd punch you in the nose." I was still in control, my threat conditional.

I'm not sure precisely what he answered. It's not that I have forgotten; that same night I wasn't word-for-word sure. But what it added up to was crystal clear. He asserted that Jews are filth and also retorted that no Jew would or could lay a hand on him, and if I thought I could to try it.

What followed will read like, and indeed was, pure Street-and-Smith pulp. I mean that "the next thing I knew," his hands were up to his face and my right fist was withdrawing from his suddenly red cheek. Conscious now that I had actually punched him, I became conscious too that my head, my heart, even my arms and legs were one furious furnace of hate and that I would consume him in it. "I followed with a left," and "he started going down." The helplessness of his crumbling fueled rather than appeased me and I pummeled more punches onto his head.

Suddenly in the Sunday morning quiet, like an off-stage chorus on cue, there sounded shouts of "Stop him!" but no one did.

They should have stopped me. All that they knew was that a younger man was beating up an older man, but this is New York, where Kitty Genovese lived and was publicly murdered. Now he lay before me, hands covering his head. I kicked his legs aside, stepped over him and started toward the nearby candy store.

The "chorus," some six, maybe eight, early risers, was grouped in front of the store. As a kind of rationale in response to their cries moments ago of "Stop him!" and also, I remember thinking, to allay the fear of me in their eyes, I boomed, "He's an anti-Semite. Called me a stinking Jew." They said nothing, and as in a scene from a Western movie when the bad guy moves toward the barroom's swinging doors, they parted to make way for me as I strode into the candy store.

Inside were the two owners and a young man who seemed to be the son of one of them. I said *"Times"* to the youth; he handed one to me and looked, I remember imagining, sympathetic. Again my voice, in explanation rather than reportage: "He called you all stinking Jews. He's turning people away from you—because you're Jewish." The owner, on my, the customer's, side of the counter, answered in a half whisper, "Shh, lower it." I recall thinking, not contemptuously, but just thinking, that he didn't want the chorus, now reformed at the door, to know that they were Jews! Then, as I was paying the owner behind the counter, he spoke. In a voice too loud, a voice pitched for hearing by the chorus behind me, he more declared than said, "We're not Jews!"

An hour or so later, back in my apartment I received a long distance call from my brother. We must have talked for ten minutes and I never once mentioned what had happened. I had completely forgotten it!

Of course it returned after I hung up, and my wife and I that day and for days thereafter, hashed and re-hashed, analyzed and dissected my wild morning minutes.

Were the candy store people really not Jewish? I didn't give a damn. It was irrelevant. If they were and were hiding it, I also didn't care. They were merely props, not *dramatis personnae* in what happened.

Something else. I knew that very afternoon that had I been walking a street in Greenwich Village, or Brooklyn Heights, or anywhere other than German Yorkville, and the same man said the same thing in the same accent, I'd never have responded as I did. Under such circumstances, it somehow wouldn't have mattered, not all that much. And even in Yorkville, had the same man said the same thing but in a French or an English accent, it also would never have burst into what it did. The combustibles, the *only* combustibles, were a German-accented anti-Semite in Germantown.

I also thought about his age. I said mid-fifties, but for all that I actually knew, he might have been sixty. What of the morality of a 44-year-old beating up a man nearly eligible for Social Security? I thought about it, but I had no problem with it. This is the way my mind ran, and in-deed runs: Why should his age have been his shield? Did sixty-year-old Nazis disqualify themselves from acting against Jews? Or for that matter, were eighteen-year-old Nazis to be absolved of their crimes because they were "too young to understand"? And 35-year-old Nazis, should they have been fought with a turned cheek because they were breadwinners for warm and loving families? No, I had no problem with what I had done and in a satisfied, almost peaceful frame of mind conjectured that I'd have beaten the hell out of him if he were seventy!

The question begs itself in the writing of this as it did in the thinking of it. What if he had been a burly, younger man? Would I have reacted as I did? I think I would have. More candidly, less "modestly," I know I would have.

But there were less academic questions, questions of chilling realism. When in two minutes I left the candy store, he had already gone. What if he had still been there, unconscious or dead? What if in falling he had hit his head and been killed? Or if he had a bad heart? I thought about that and about my career and about my wife. The end line of my thought, however, was that had I ignored the man, his face and his words, I'd have felt worse—longer.

Mel Ott, Zorba the Greek,
a Nightmare

Tell Me It Isn't True, Honey. The Kazant-
sakis summer. The final legacy of the dying
master. Their hooked noses dripped venom.
Scratch a goy. Imagine!

As a young man, I felt warmly about Voltaire, but the New
York Giants' home run king, Mel Ott, aside, if I had any
favorite hero it was Jack London. I saw him as I did Voltaire, brilliant, entrancingly readable, and a derring-doer
on the side of social justice. I was at that age when Causes
were supplanting box scores as the things that really mattered. Later, somewhat along in both my readings and my
causes, my love was spurned. It turned out that Voltaire
and London had more than social justice in common. Voltaire was a part-time anti-Semite, London a racist. All
these years when I have thought about it, I've been
pleased by the fading of London's fame; it serves him
right. And I eagerly read any and all rationalizations of
Voltaire's anti-Semitism; I want to believe he didn't
really mean it. I suppose it's a case of, Tell Me It Isn't
True, Honey. On the other hand, Mel Ott, whose furthest
horizon, for all I know, was the right field fence at the
Polo Grounds, never once let me down.

All of which is by way of an introduction to one of my

41

adulthood's maximum heroes, Nikos Kazantsakis. As one remembers a boyhood summer in camp, or summer standing for the first time before the Grand Canyon, or summer driving through the French and Italian countryside, I remember the summer my wife and I read aloud to each other Kazantsakis' *The Odyssey: A Modern Sequel.* We read it evenings sprawled on our shag rug neath the beamed ceiling of our living room, we read it to each other on Florida beaches, we read and we read, and all the while our voices dubbed Ulysses' exaltation of life, we were falling in love with Kazantsakis.

It was no summer romance, but alas, neither was our beloved a man for all seasons. I had gone on to *Zorba the Greek,* then *The Greek Passion, Freedom or Death, The Last Temptation of Christ,* devouring the Man-God's controlled artistry, the contagion of his free and his full heart, liberating my own. When his posthumously published autobiography, *Report to Greco,* was available in the United States, I rushed to buy, to own and to treasure the final legacy of the dying master. And it was a single line, a sentence as swift and as sudden as a karate blow that snapped my adoration. Not philosophy, not poetry, just workaday words strung plainly together, describing a Jerusalem street scene casually glanced a lifetime ago. The sentence told of a winding street his young manhood's eyes had beheld, and now the old man's reminiscences recalled that, "The Jews, with their long greasy sideburns, slunk along the walls of the houses, their hooked noses dripping venom."

I don't mean to make a big thing out of this, out of the "greasy" sideburns, the "hooked noses dripping venom." Nor do I want to suggest that, Scratch a Goy, even a Good One, and you'll Find an Anti-Semite. I not only don't believe that, but readily confess to still feeling a mixture of awe and rapture in reading Kazantsakis, still think of him as a Man-God. Besides, who says that God Himself is altogether free of anti-Semitism?

But I do have a point in all this and it's the flash of insight into European anti-Semitism that Kazantsakis' *Report to Greco* gave me.

Earlier in the book, recalling his young boyhood, he wrote:

"The sound of certain words excited me terribly—it was fear I felt most often, not joy. Especially Hebrew words, for I knew from my grandmother that on Good Friday the Jews took Christian children and tossed them into a trough lined with spikes and drank their blood. Oftentimes it seemed to me that a Hebrew word from the Old Testament was a spike lined trough and that someone wanted to throw me in."

A Cretan boy and his nightmare. A million boys, millions of boys, each of them and all of them nightmared by Jews. Tow headed German children, blond Polish children, chubby Austrian children, all of them growing older, all of them nightmare haunted. Suddenly they are men, boys grown older, but still men and their fear has turned to resentment, and muscled now and shrewder they have available recourse more fitting manhood than their grandmother's protecting bosom.

Imagine! The crematoria were committed in self-defense. They were an old score finally settled. Incredible!

More Roman than the Romans

We were living in Miami Beach. "How was school today?" Crazy names. A thirteen year old's innocence. An adult's innocence.

I used to tell this story for laughs but the truth is that I derived from it a kind of Star-Spangled pride.

We were living in Miami Beach when Castro took over Cuba. When the refugees began pouring into Miami my daughter was thirteen years old and in junior high school. One dinnertime, in response to my serviceable, if uninspired, parental conversation opener: "How was school today?" she replied that there were now over forty Cuban children in her school.

"Really?"

"Yes, and they have such crazy names, Menendes, Morales, Gonzales . . ." She paused, and then, thoughtfully, "but some of them have American names . . . Goldstein, Schwartz."

My audiences, being largely first-generation American, had personal memories of the sometime burden of a Jewish name in years past. Their laughter was in response to my daughter's innocence, but their pleasure was in the recognition that for all that our sons and daughters are less harriedly Jewish than we were, they are also more relaxedly American. And although the story was about the innocence of a child, my intended message was of Melting Pots and of an America that has been good.

America has indeed been good, but the innocence was mine. So nervously American are we, that in gladness that our children are not, I missed the real point of my own story. My daughter didn't even know she was Jewish!

More accurately, she didn't *feel* Jewish, and if you don't feel Jewish how can you *be* Jewish?

There's a relevant quote attributed to Jan Masaryk. He was deploring the low key of patriotism in pre-World War II Czechoslovakia. "Czechs are for the Czechs and Slavs for the Slavs. No one is for Czechoslovakia—except for the Jews. They are our only Czechoslovakians."

Jews used to repeat that quotation boastfully and, I suspect, propagandistically. The intended-to-please nervous chatter of an unpacked guest hoping to stay. He's more Roman than the Romans, more Communist than the Communists. Understandable, but today there are still Czechs in Czechoslovakia, and still Slavs in Czechoslovakia, but there aren't many Jews left.

The story of my little girl was more sad than it was funny.

Soul

Jews and Negroes, too, are dissolving. The stomach as fourteen carats. Blacks don't much give a damn. Fed and forty, we are liberated and objective. Jewish soul.

Dr. Bernard Lander, professor of sociology . . . contended that indifference to Israel registered "by a considerable proportion of Jewish college students in the late 1950's is now being transformed into outright hostility."

Israel, he said, "is part of the Establishment" and "is a major target of hate and attack by the New Left, which in the main is being led by youths of Jewish background.

"It is becoming commonplace," he added, "for Jewish youths to sell Al Fatah stamps on college campuses and for young men and women of excellent Jewish homes to preach New Left propaganda of hate of Israel."
—New York Times, November 29, 1969

Needless to say, these young people do not consider themselves anti-Semitic, do consider themselves objective. This "objectivity" about ethnicity is why Jews, and Negroes too, are dissolving while blacks are taking shape. Blacks are defining themselves and Jews, like Negroes, are no longer quite sure who they are. Jews and Negroes have in common that they talk of right and wrong. Not much group identity in that. Blacks, like Mrs. Peachum, bellow, "First feed the face, then talk to me of right and wrong." There, right smack in the pit of the stomach, is fourteen carat group identity.

Blacks don't much give a damn about your attitude toward race. Their point, a strategically good one, is that it's not nearly so important as the effect of your behavior on the poor and on the politically powerless, for poverty and powerlessness are the *de facto* definitions of race.

But Jews no longer ask each other if the mugged merchant was Jewish. "What difference does his religion make?" Fed and forty, we are liberated from our groupness and have become objective. That's why, when blacks were solidly for Ocean Hill's school administration in New York's teacher strike and most Negroes were discreetly silent, Jews split. Blacks responded to where black was at: "the community."

Jews, on the other hand, cerebrated, despite the fact that the *de facto* definition of "New York school teacher" is Jew. Similarly many Jewish liberals have yet to voice rhetoric in behalf of ghetto merchants which either compares, in decibel or indignation, with their statements on the "urban problem."

This despite their knowing—and everybody else knowing—that "merchant," and "elderly white tenement-dweller" are, in New York, *de facto* synonyms for Jew.

Ghetto-locked, we Jews had a *Yiddishe neshuma.* We're free now of the ghetto but we left our soul feeling behind. It's not languishing. It's alive and well and living with our successors there, and only its name is changed: black soul. In its place the *Times* story's Jews have objectivity, and who ever heard of building a nation, a culture, or even a good softball team, on objectivity?

Radical Styles; the Why
of the Difference

*A drink is not an ice cream soda. Virginity
and radicalism. Jews as a special kind of
people with fixed qualities. Jews not as a
special kind of people with fixed qualities.
Who'd have thought it would lead to this.*

I was nineteen, several days a clerk-typist at the War Department in Washington, D.C., when a co-worker stopped
by my desk to say to me that some of us are stopping for a
drink after work, would you like to join us? I had made no
friends and so gratefully but nonchalantly said, Yeh, sure.
At five, eight of us, four men and four girls, left our Con-
stitutional Avenue office and headed, walking, downtown.
We passed a Peoples' Drug Store where I had had an ice-
cream soda one lunchtime, and I offered, This is a good
place. My new friends chuckled. Something, I figured,
they know that I don't about Peoples'. Walking further,
we approached an ice-cream parlor, and I asked How
about this place? It was at this point that they surmised
that I had not been playing the comedian back by Peoples', that I had meant what I said. For my part, it dawned
on me that when they invited me to a drink they meant
liquor. Until that night, the only alcohol I had ever had
was at weddings, and on Jewish holy days, and a drink

51

meant a chocolate, or maybe a raspberry, ice-cream soda. I was, although I didn't then know it, a walking statistic, testimony to the fact that Jews were not drinkers.

Nineteen year old Jews and the statistics of them, too, are changing. A survey of college youths revealed that 63 percent of the Protestants and 57 percent of the Catholics reported they had never used marijuana. However, only 32 percent of the Jewish youths responded, Never. Twenty four percent of Jewish youths admitted to frequent smoking of marijuana, fully three times the number of Protestant and Catholic frequent users of pot.

I don't know what the intercourse graph for my generation of Jewish youth looked like, but whiskey wasn't the only thing I was to experience for the first time at nineteen. Today's youth is not only faster, but racier too. The survey goes on to reveal that among youths who use pot often, 43 percent of the males engage in frequent intercourse, and 86 percent of the females report occasional or frequent sexual intercourse. In view of the dominant presence of Jews among pot users, it would seem that the stereotype of the Jew as non-athletic has finally been overcome.

As radicals, the current generation of Jewish youth seems to be carrying on a family tradition, at least at first blush. Nathan Glazer has reported that only a tiny fraction of the Jewish student body of our campuses are radicals, but that among radical students, the percentage of Jews is higher, proportionately, than the percentage of non-Jews. I suspect that a like study in the 1930's or early 1940's would have revealed that the percentage of Jews who were Communists made for a sparse platoon, but that the small Communist Party nonetheless had a decided Yiddish accent.

But alas, as college beer and virginity have gone to

pot, radicalism has too. I mean more than the statistical relationship between radicalism and the use of marijuana. I mean the difference between reading the *Daily Worker*, or talk-talk-talking in red Union Square in the 1930's, and today's fire-bombing of college buildings, banks, and armories. It's the difference between reason, even foolish reasoning, and murder, even reasoned murder.

Why? Our generation's radicals were outsiders, so viewed by a society that discriminated against them socially, politically, and economically, and consequently Marginal Men, they turned to radicalism as the passkey to the closed society. But today's young Jewish radicals have been born in a society whose doors their fathers opened, and holding father's coattails, they followed him in. Now, in the American Jewish Committee's *Jews in the Mind of America*, its author, Charles Stember, can report that ". . . far fewer persons than formerly think of Jews as having any distinctive traits or characteristics at all, whether good or bad. Jews, it would appear, are being perceived more and more as individuals, rather than as a special kind of people with fixed qualities."

Interestingly, I almost said sadly, and that's what I mean too, many of today's militantly radical youth have been fathered and mothered by Stember's described Jews, the acculturated made-its, not a traditionalist among them. Is this the Why of the difference in the generational expression of radicalism? That yesteryear's Socialists, labor organizers, idealizers of the Soviets, were radicals reared in the traditions of "a special people with fixed qualities" and consequently were reined by their peoplehood? And that today's radicals, reared by homogenized Jews, and so neither fully Jewish nor fully acculturated, remain Marginal Men, but without the social controls of "a special kind of people"? Is it because "perceived more and more as individuals," they are in fact more individu-alistic than we were, and so act out their unbridled per-sonal fantasies where we did our group yearnings?

I got silly drunk that night in Washington when I strayed from the graph of Jewish non-drinkers. Who'd have thought my meandering would lead to this?

Intermarriage

I could tell that she liked me too.
Sex, dreaming it, talking of it,
searching for it. Non-Jewish girls
were different. It served me right.
The No Trespassing signs are down.
"He's kind of skinny, isn't he,
dear?" I should have known better.

I remember her face, her light-reflecting, olive complexion, her Italian eyes that in my memory are two luminous black marbles, and I remember that she had the biggest and the most beautifully shaped breasts in our eighth grade. Because we had two Glorias in our class and she was the taller, we referred to her as "Big Gloria," at least when it was her name that we had in mind.

Though we hardly ever spoke to each other, we liked each other. Day dreaming her as often as I did, and not always by day, I was, of course, sure of my affection for her, but the way in which we'd both of us embarrassedly slide our eyes away when, over distances in the classroom or in the hallways, we'd catch each other looking softly at one another, I could tell that she liked me too. Even that time in the subway seat for two, the one seat at the end of the car that used to be partitioned off, when she let me fondle her breasts, we mostly kissed and looked at each other, hardly talking. We were on a class outing, visiting a museum, and I'm no longer sure whether our being seated together in that particular seat just happened, or whether by lingering while others were taking their places we separately but in concert engineered our pairing. But no matter, for all that it happened thirty-five years ago, Gloria, like an ageless figure on a Grecian urn, remains an olive complexioned nymphet, her eyes wide and black and shining, her breasts beckoning, magnetic.

I think it was that Gloria was Italian, or more accurately, that she was not Jewish, that rendered her more exotic, and me more erotic. At thirteen, I understood subliminally that Jewish girls were a pool from which one day I would choose a wife. Sex—we dreamt of it, talked of it, and searched for it—was something boys did to, not with, girls. It was a boy's pleasure, a girl's—even a willing girl's —defilement. And so we didn't, at least not often, contaminate our own pool. But non-Jewish girls were different; they were not for marrying.

Years later, in the Marine Corps, when Brooklyn Italians would recall to me their high school exploits with Jewish girls, I figured it served me right.

Which leads me to intermarriage. Its practice has become commonplace. To be sure, ethnicity is alive and well, but the No Trespassing signs are down. What has happened is that while foreigners have retained their aphrodisiacal qualities (afrodisiacal?), they are no longer viewed as lesser breeds without the law. And so today a Jewish boy doesn't marry into Christendom, he marries romantic Italy or traditioned New England, and a young gentile rather than marrying a Jew girl, joins himself with the warmth and mysteries of a five thousand year old culture. More critical today of our own traditions, I mean all of us, we are also more accepting of other cultures. It may be that too long, too uncritical of our own, we are now overly critical, and too long, too intolerant of others, we are now overly accepting. Also, sex, indeed marriage itself, being less holy today, they are less sinful too. In today's freer times, likely were I now thirteen, I'd have met Gloria openly, met her parents and she mine.

But I am not thirteen, and I am certainly not of the now generation; rather am I a then thirteen year old, grown a quarter century older. And my daughter is married to a non-Jew.

They're happily married and for this I am happy, but their courting and engagement wasn't easy. That is, for me. The vague apprehension I felt when first they began seeing each other grew thicker with their dating; my responses, heavier. I offered pretendedly casual suggestions that she date other boys. Then you'll know if you really love him. (That really meant, why don't you try Jewish boys?) Invitingly, I suggested, How'd you like a vacation this summer in Europe? (That really meant, maybe a Time Out will snap the rally.) One day, embarrassed for myself even as I was saying it, I commented on how odd looking a couple they made, He's kind of skinny, isn't he, dear? (And that really meant, transparently, I'm afraid, Don't marry him: he's not Jewish.)

Finally, too late, too late by some twenty years of preachments on the fundamental equality of all peoples, Race-and-Religion-don't-really-matter, You've-gotta-judge-a-person-by-what-he-himself-is, I broached the subject head on, indirectly. I spoke to her of the thousands of years of Jewish continuity, of the miracle of that continuity, and clumsily paraphrasing a Leslie Fiedler short story protagonist, asked her what right any Jew had to say, Stop, I'm getting off, Enough of this Jewish continuity, I quit.

Of course she didn't see herself as quitting the Jewish people, no more than my generation of rationalist Jews saw itself as leaving Judaism, no matter that our elders mourned our synagogue absence. She married the young man, and her deed done, if I bear him any hostility it's that he's such a nice boy, and so deprives me of the pain I was prepared to nurture.

I write of it lightly now, much as we recall pain without pain. But there was crisis. The moment in which your daughter drops her eyes and shielding you from the hardness of her resolution by voicing it softly, she says, Daddy, I love him, We are getting married, and the way in which she enunciates "are" is your moment of crisis. We decided, my wife and I, without ever discussing it, just by our responses, that the reality of the continuity of our parent-child relationship meant more to us than the continuity of our line in Israel. In the end, it was that elemental.

Something else about our reactions, or more specifically, about my mother's. To our surprise, my mother, for whom gentiles, any gentiles, conjure images of drunken Polish peasants, accepted my daughter's marriage intentions far more readily than did we. I think I know why. It's related to something I despairingly thought when we suspected but did not yet know that the kids would get married. One day, sensing defeat and awash in self-pity, I consoled myself with, after we're dead and gone, What difference will it make? Maybe my mother, having lived longer, for being less a stranger to thoughts of mortality than we her children, understood this sooner and better than we did. I think so.

But still I should have known better, sooner. I should have known because of that subway ride with Gloria on our eighth grade school outing. We were on our way to the Museum of Natural History.

Old Soldiers

My profession problemed my mother. What do you say? More for show than for sale. What kind of life is that, for a nice Jewish boy? Victory happened.

My profession problemed my mother. To be sure, she had an intuitive respect for the Anti-Defamation League, and if she didn't really know very much about its activities, the mere fact that I was associated with ADL certified its respectability. Her problem was not with what I was doing, but rather with how to describe what *her* son does, when meeting her contemporaries, and exchanging (really, matching) reports on the doings of "the children." What *do* you say when Mrs. Bloom has reported that her son is a doctor, Mrs. Feinstein that hers is an accountant? Do you offer, as my mother would have had to, that yours "fights anti-Semitism"? That's a profession? So she didn't. She'd say My Nathan's a lawyer. A lawyer I am, but lawyering I wasn't. To her and to her generation of poor and unschooled immigrant Jews, being a lawyer, or a doctor, an accountant, or a dentist, a *professional*, suggested Education, and more, it suggested a tangible, recognized accomplishment. Something you could prove by hanging up a shingle. I think too that our parents in

America were not as impressed with the importance of "fighting anti-Semitism" as we were. After all, memoried in Europe, American forms of anti-Semitism must have seemed like *kinder-shpiel* to them.

In my twenties, when I was with the ADL in Colorado and my "territory" included New Mexico, Wyoming and Utah, where travellers in trains and planes tended to readier conversation with seat neighbors than back East, I had a problem. The man next to me seemed always to be a salesman and following brief openers about the weather, the countryside, or where you from, he'd say he sells this or that, you sell too? "I'm in human relations," or "I'm in intergroup relations," I'd fudge, and if pressed, I'd explain that the Anti-Defamation League was a Jewish sponsored organization trying to bring about the brotherhood of man, under the Fatherhood of God. The words, sticky in my throat, never came easily, but blessedly—I dislike small-talking—they usually dried my neighbor's talking tap, and soon we'd both be returned to our lapped *Life* or *Look*.

Of course, the direct, comprehensible answer would have been, "I fight against the institutions of anti-Semitism; I try to effect the passage of civil rights laws." I couldn't say this, not to strangers, because undoing anti-Semitism and Jim Crow was a mission with me, so deeply felt that I had committed my career to it. To buckshot small talk about my life's work and at a random stranger, was to somehow imbue my private mission with the texture of a public Crusade, and I was and am incapable of loving, or for that matter, bleeding in public; of being, in short, a Missionary. In a way, not unrelated to my mother's, my surface truth about what I was doing was more for show than it was for sale.

I want to return to my mother now, as a bridge to the

real point concerning myself and my work. There is an old joke that Jews tell on themselves. It has several Jewish mothers discussing the accomplishments of their grown sons. One reports that her son is a doctor, and what's more, he has an elegant office on Park Avenue. The ladies are appropriately impressed. Another reports that her son is an attorney and has a suite of offices on Wall Street in which he employs a staff of thirty-five other attorneys. Again, murmured approbation. The third mother, feeling somewhat outflanked by these reports of the material success of her friends' children, lamely but bravely offers up that her son is a rabbi. The punch line has one of the other ladies, one whose son has "made it," ask incredulously, "What kind of life is *that*, for a nice Jewish boy?"

Of late, this story has been echoing in my thoughts, but without chuckles, and hearing it in thought, I am unsmiled. I cared deeply for my work, felt, in the language currently fashionable, "relevant." Now, or for now, it is largely over. Anti-Semitism in America, the socially sanctioned variety, is a battle largely won. The American anti-Semite today must camouflage his feelings, so unfashionable has the old anti-Semitism become. Civil rights too are a rolling, growing snowball, ably accelerated by Negroes.

And now while middle aged doctor-sons continue to doctor, and middle aged lawyer-sons continue to lawyer, am I, these my years of experience, this my talent sharply honed, to continue fighting routed and retreating anti-Semites, like some tragi-comic General crying, *Charge!*, long after the war's been won? I was girded for a lifetime's struggle when suddenly, unexpectedly, victory happened.

And so, for the nonce, I am emotionally unemployed, and that indeed is no life for a nice, albeit getting on, Jewish boy.

The Meter and Max's
Nervous Ears

*He owned downtown. Direct from a Long
Run in the Old Testament. Mr. Johnson
bought the store with Mr. Cohen's good
will. They aren't returning to Spanish
Moss. The diaspora within the diaspora.
God is alive and well. Why we must wish
Them well.*

Max Goldfarb had been a peddler in the 1920's and for all
that he was a young man, he was tiring of the road and so
he settled down in Brook City, opened a dry goods store,
and when I knew him in the late 1950's he owned downtown. Brook City had a population then of approximately
ten thousand, or as they like to say in small Southern
towns, ten thousand souls. Everyone knew Max and Max
knew most everyone. He was more an integrated member
of the social life of Brook City, its Club, its service organi-
zations, its Chamber of Commerce, than the Jewish merchant princes I have known in the cosmopolitan North.

On the particular day I have in mind, a relentlessly
hot August afternoon, Max was chauffeuring me down the
four block length of Main Street, stopping and parking,
starting again, stopping and parking again, so that he
might introduce me to the four Jewish merchants on the

street. Max was a member of B'nai B'rith, I was with its
Anti-Defamation League and the introductions were for
fund-raising purposes. At each store, I'd engage in conversation with Max's fellow townsman and because the
parking meter sold time by the minutes, Max was peri-
odically leaving us to pay it its pennies. Finally, on the
third stop, seeing that the back and forth walks in the hot
sun were tiring him, I remonstrated, why are you running
back and forth so much? To hell with the dollar fine, and
take it easy, Max, it's too hot. His answer is one of the
points I want to make. "It's all right, I don't want them
to think that the Jew has so much money he doesn't give
a damn."

Max taught bible class in the Brook City Baptist
Church's Sunday School. Live. Direct from a Long Run in
the Old Testament. Christian acceptance real enough,
and Max was pleased with it, almost boastful of it. But
no matter, after a lifetime in Brook City, the running
meter was still Theirs and Max's ears were still nervous.

Driving through Cypresstown in the 1950's, I saw a
dry goods store called *Cohen's* and thought I'd introduce
myself to Cohen, maybe learn something of the town,
maybe even make a friend for the ADL, so I stopped in. I
asked the man for Mr. Cohen and he said, My name's
Johnson. Bill Johnson. Help you?

I'm looking for Mr. Cohen.

Mr. Cohen's gone, lives in Jacksonville, I think. This
is my place. Bought it from Mr. Cohen eight years ago.
Help you?

My face must have registered my puzzlement because
he picked up again. "The sign's still *Cohen's* 'cause I
bought the store with Mr. Cohen's good will."

Not far from Cypresstown there's a sun drenched
city much like it. I had a friend there—ready-to-wear

men's clothes—with whom I discussed the wonder, to me, of a Johnson, in a Cypresstown, calling his place *Cohen's,* and for business reasons! My friend explained, "We get along fine here. No trouble. Oh, once in a while you hear something, but if we mind our own business, they leave us alone. We get along fine."

In the small towns of the South, Jews do "get along fine." They've prospered, prided in being "accepted," raised families, sent their children to college, and importantly for them, their sons and daughters, by and large, know who they are—Jews.

But they've paid a price for getting along fine. It's been minding their own business, not being like, or seeming to be like, those New York Jews. For their children who have been off to college—virtually all of them—this asking price is too high, and so they aren't returning to Spanish Moss; instead, they're settling in the big city, Miami, Birmingham, Atlanta, New Orleans, or maybe up North. Even for himself, Cohen never intended to stay, or, more accurately, die, in Cypresstown. He viewed the price he paid—"minding our own business"—as rent, and now that the kids have moved and have their own families, he's leaving his rental, his Club, his Kiwanis, his Chamber, and he's moving to Jacksonville to be near the grandchildren, and to die among Jews.

That price he paid, conformity, seems dearer to an intellectual than likely it was to him. But intellectuals didn't settle in Spanish Moss. The towns and villages of the South were settled in by security minded Jews, loners, men who wanted to be their own boss and so became storekeepers. They stopped in New York or in Philadelphia enroute from Russia and finding economic gall rather than gold in the streets, they moved on, to the West, the Southwest, the Rocky Mountain States, the mid-West, the Northeast, throughout all of America, the proverbial pack on their back, seeking and searching for a place "to make a living." Theirs was a diaspora within the diaspora. Ironically, these strange soils preserved them as identifying and identifiable Jews.

I said that they know who they are. Life in small towns where Jews number a score, a *minyan*, sometimes less, makes for being consciously Jewish in a way unknown to New Yorkers, to residents of Miami Beach, to Jews in the Jewish sections of big cities. There's no forgetting that you are Jewish in Spanish Moss, because your total environment is Christian. Point and counterpoint, with customers in the Jew store, with Christian friends who look to you as an authority on the Old Testament, and on Sundays, walking Sunday-dressed Main Street. Some days you know you are Jewish because of anti-Semitism. Nothing new there. But some days you know it because of philo-Semitism. Baptist: "We don't abuse our Jewish folks. Oughtn't nobody abuse them 'cause they're here to save us."

And sometimes your day in, day out, awareness that you are Jewish is buoyed by neither hostility nor friendship, but innocence: "Mr. Goldman, you a Protestant Jew or a Catholic Jew?" Or the question asked of a Jewish teacher at a junior college in central Florida: "Can you be Jewish and an American too?" Or the Sunday School teacher who asked her class, "Who killed Jesus?" and the six year old who answered brightly, "Mr. Silverman."

In rural America the Jew's visibility to Christians has caused him to become visible to himself. His Christian neighbors knowing who they were, he had to know—in order to stand tall—who he was. Besides, they expected it of him. In a way, then, it was necessary to remain Jewish, for Their sake, to meet Their expectations. As a result, his reading in Jewish history, his indoctrination of his children with a sense of the tradition into which they had been born, his sense of his Jewish identity, like a used muscle, grew, while his unused self—the secular man in all of us—the part of us that wants to dissent from stifling or insensitive conformity, atrophied.

But walk down New York's Fifth Avenue, Miami Beach's Lincoln Road, Chicago's Michigan Avenue, and your awareness of your Jewishness is as distant from your consciousness as the color of your eyes. The walk is your strolling self's rather than your Jewish self's, the purchase you make is a transaction of strangers, your Jewishness, her gentleness dormant, even as your eyes meet. And when you are in a Jewish neighborhood, because all of your world is Jewish, none of you are. So it is that in New York one's Jewishness is often an unexercised muscle while one's secularity, for being in free use, grows.

I sometimes think that it's been Christianity that's preserved us as a people apart. But something is happening. Young gentiles today aren't as anti-Semitic as their parents were. They aren't as Christian either, and the connection is to wonder. The abatement of anti-Semitism in America has coincided with the increasing talk of the death of God. Likely God is alive and well, somewhere, and it's Christianity that is dying—its conceit causing it to mourn God rather than itself.

For Jews it all poses a problem. It's been easier to be Jewish for Christians, than for ourselves. We must wish them well, else what will become of us?

Southerners and Jews

Consider the word, Yankee. In the South, history is for the masses. Southerners suggest Jews and northerners, gentiles. Northerners as tourists.

Southerners consider themselves as Southerners, and northerners view them that way too, but not the other way around. I mean while Southerners consider northerners Northerners, northerners don't think of themselves as Northerners. New Englanders, yes, Midwesterners, yes, but not Northerners. The difference in outlook, or maybe it's inlook, has more to do with mind than with maps. Southerners are losers, and what losers share in common knits them tighter together than what winners share in common. Alabamans feel closer to Mississippians than do New Yorkers to Pennsylvanians. Or consider the word Yankee. When Southerners use it they are remembering the Civil War, sour tasting its regurgitations. When a Bay Stater or a Vermonter says Yankee, he is invoking, not experiencing, a memory, and even then it's of another war, the Revolutionary War, book-taught rather than grandfather taled. In the South, history is for the masses, for their study and their handing down. In the North it's for history buffs and for Pilgrim nostalgia. It's like in poker. Winners tell jokes; losers say, Deal.

Southerners suggest Jews and northerners, gentiles. But for all that Jews see gentiles as gentiles, gentiles are not aware of themselves as gentiles, but rather as Baptists or Lutherans, etc.

More. In the South there are Sons of the Confederacy, Daughters of the Confederacy, Societies for the Preservation of Southern Traditions, Louisiana variations on the themes, Mississippi variations, Florida variations, on and on and on. But has anyone yet found one organization designed to preserve the Northern Way of Life?

And so with Jews. B'nai B'rith, Hadassah, Mizrachi, National Council of Jewish Women, Jewish War Veterans, American Jewish Committee, American Jewish Congress, American—and there are so few Jews! I sometimes think as I visit from organization to organization and more often than not see the same faces, that we Jews invented interlocking directorates—how else would there be enough of us to go around?

And I have noticed too, that when a northerner travels South, he's touristing, but when a Southerner travels north, he enters the diaspora.

The Six Day War

When Israel was born. "Real" Jews and
the other kind. Menasha Skulnik and
Charlton Heston. Panic and prayer.
Transistor walking Manhattan. All at
once, all together.

The older I've grown, the more my heart and my mind
have become absorbed with the security and the well being of Israel. In 1948 when Israel was born, I was glad because the displaced Jews of Europe now had a place to go
to. That was the level and the depth of my response, gladness. I was twenty-five. Israel then and for almost a score
of years thereafter represented for me a sanctuary for refugees. I had no feelings of a "Jewish homeland," and certainly none of a biblically prophesized homecoming.
Indeed, on a would-you-rather-visit list, Israel ranked behind Paris, England, Japan, each of which evoked in me a
sense of history, culture, and the exotic, more stirring than
my responses to geographical Israel.

And when I have retained consciousness of them as
Jews rather than as Israelis, the Israelis whom I've met
have reached me as cousin Jews, rather than as brother
Jews. I suppose it's because for me, "real" Jews come either from urban America or from Russian or Polish ghet-

toes. Of course, I have extended diplomatic recognition and deported myself with civility to other Jews, but the truth is that before I fully accept them, I must get past their small town ways, or their French accent or their British dress. And so it is with the Israelis. They're "different." Their accents are neither New York nor the Pale, they often behave more like Charlton Heston than Menasha Skulnik, and those proud, somewhat smug, *sabras* are more suggestive of the First Families of Virginia than the Workman's Circle. Besides, by me, Yiddish is Jewish and Hebrew, a foreign language.

But 1967's Six Day War changed everything. In an hour, in a moment really, in the time it took to hear the radio voice announcing War, I became one with my transistor, mind and *neshuma* suddenly, without premonition, frightened hosts to entangled panic and prayer. The revelations of the crematoria did not affect me so cataclysmically. Then a part of me was wrung, defiled, deadened. But I was on top of it, alive to cry, to hate, to mourn, to go on. Besides we learned of Auschwitz after the fact. But now The Fact, the possibility of Israel's decimation, Yes? No? was teetering in tense, a prospective nation murder happening half way around the world, and transistor walking Manhattan, my own life, all that I was and all that I might be, teetered too. But more than the draining of my own meaning, infinitely more, Israel's murder would be a remorseless sentence of WORTHLESS passed on millenia of Jewish life, aborting, irrevocably, Jewish tomorrows.

Those were my reactions. They were the reactions of millions of us. Jews whose messengers were Japanese transistors, Jews whose starved for news was filtered them by Tass, religious Jews, atheist Jews, chauvinistic Jews and indifferent Jews, New York Jews and Wyoming Jews, all, as if responding to a race recalled Alert, a signal as old as

Abraham himself, stopping their lives dead still, waiting, awed and fearful, for the news, Israel lives? Yes? No?

Why this extraordinary response? I have said that Israel's death in rendering futile Jewish yesterdays and barren our tomorrows, was our individual death too. Is this the why of our reactions? I am not really sure. I simply relate what I felt, what so many others felt, all at once, all together.

LEFT, RIGHT. LEFT, RIGHT

Before I begin what I want to say, I want to say something. Where I lived in Williamsburg as a boy, the Democrats were a plurality, and it was my impression that close behind them, at least in decibel count, were the Communists and various Socialist factions. Republicans were as numerous as Whigs. When I say Democrats, I should explain. They were Democrats who yes, they believed in Socialism, but Roosevelt is good for Jews, good for the worker, and besides, a vote for the Socialists is a wasted vote. So Socialism had our respect and the Democrats had our votes. For it was Roosevelt who seemed hawkish toward the Nazis, Roosevelt who led us out of the Great Depression, and it was Mrs. Roosevelt who spoke to our plaintiff's pursuit of civil rights. Besides, our districts' office holders often being Jews, the Democratic Party looked Jewish. Conversely, the Republican Party looked gentile.

During the elections of 1970, I met an old friend, one whom I had known for more than twenty-five years as a voting booth Democrat and a living room Socialist. We talked family, old times, and some politics. On the latter, he offered, "I've been a lifelong Republican . . . the past six months." Of course, he was half joking. Half, I said.

It's the half of me that is defecting that I write of here, no matter my subject matter includes huge red phalluses, schnapps and beer chasers, country music, blacks, World War II, some this and some that. Not defection from Democrat to Republican. That's a short walk and hardly worth talking about. Rather, my straying, hardly aware along the way the distance I was traveling, from Left to (the word comes haltingly) Right.

How did it happen? Self interest. The same kind of self interest that in the 1930's turned me Left, in the 1960's turned me Right.

But I am making too much of Left and Right and the implied distance in between. Perhaps all that I mean to say is that what discomforts me in the Left today, is hauntingly familiar. It frightened me as a boy when I discerned it in the Right.

79

Ronald Reagan and
Papist Treachery

You could almost see the huge Red phalluses. God was good. Reagan equals Hitler, Reagan equals Hitler. Back in the tabernacle.

I lived in Colorado in 1949 and in the early 50's and so did a "Reverend" who stocked his trade with anti-Communism and anti-Catholicism. He was also *pro patria.*

His audiences mainly religious fundamentalists, thirty, on a good night maybe forty in attendance, came to hear his fearlessly revealed TRUTH about COMMUNISM in OUR NATION'S CAPITOL, and about PAPIST TREACHERY. He instructed them on the RED MENACE and alerted them to the WHORE OF BABYLON and buttressed his points with heretofore OFFICIALLY REPRESSED EVIDENCE. Among his sermons was one, a beaut, in which he described rapes of Spanish nuns by Communist troops during the Spanish Civil War. He was so explicit you could almost see the huge Red phalluses sundering the poor nuns.

His congregants loved it. Imagine, passing righteous judgment on the Communist anti-Christ and simultaneously—vicariousness their prophylaxis—hate-screwing his Whore. God was good.

I think of them when I see America spelled with a *k*, as in the German Amerika. And in my memory's eye I saw them again on a TV news sequence showing hundreds of students massed in front of a hotel in which Governor Ronald Reagan was at a meeting. Their right arms extended in the Nazi salute, the students were mockingly chanting, *SIEG HEIL!*, *SIEG HEIL!*, *SIEG HEIL!* Animated hyperbole, rhythmically, insistently, declaring Reagan equals Hitler, Reagan equals Hitler, Reagan equals Hitler, and all the while they were indulging their freedoms of speech and assembly, they were frustrating the Governor's. What I mean when I say they reminded me of the Colorado pietists is that the students too seemed to be pleasuring in their indignation, in damning Reagan for their own fantasies.

Back there in the tabernacle, those wet dreaming, nun screwing Christians had become the Communist hordes, and on my TV screen the Left had become what it always warned us the Right will be.

They were also *pro patria*, or if it makes any difference, *pro publico*.

I Liked the Nazi

Several years ago, in Cologne, schnapps and beer chasers. The Germans were good conversationalists. He did his thing.

Recently, several young people invaded the International Affairs Center at Harvard. They ransacked it and roughed up clerks and secretaries, some of whom were middle-aged women. Subsequently the invaders declared that their assault on the Center's personnel was intended to convey some small sense of the far more heinous brutality the U.S. is visiting upon the Vietnamese. The Weathermen's end: peace. Their means: violence.

That incident and scores of similar ones involving young people whose idealism frequently mitigates judgment of their violence, recalls to me a night, several years ago, in Cologne.

I was winding up a month's tour of schools and Army bases, observing, as a member of an Anti-Defamation League mission, the Federal Republic's democratization program. On this particular night, the business of the mission over with, I was the guest of a high-ranking democratization officer. A friend of his, in the same program, was present and our conversation of cabbages, kings and the state of the world was generously lubricated by schnapps and beer chasers. The Germans were good conversationalists, good drinkers, and both of them had a value system that was socially compassionate and politically liberal. Both had been Nazis.

At one point one of them spoke of the condition of the Negro in the American South. His words were sensitive and they were wise and as I sat there considering him, his gentle features became blurred and as in a double exposure, they receded and emerged in alternating focus with the man as a Nazi officer.

"How come with all of these values you were a Nazi?" My voice, probably thick, was conversational, not that of an adversary. I liked him.

Softly, like my own, conversationally—he too was too schnappsed to dissemble—"I was an idealist."

The intervening years have been sobering. Likely he was an idealist. In an imperfect, perhaps even rotting Weimar Republic he yearned for a Germany pure of purpose and for Germans pure of mind, and so like the idealistic Weathermen, he did his thing.

Somewhere I once read: "There are no ends. There are only means."

Chivalry and Sadism

I attended a Ku Klux Klan meeting. "Nigger, he black on the outside, white on the inside. Jew, he white on the outside, black on the inside." Passing the sugar.

Some years ago, in the middle Fifties, I attended a Ku Klux Klan meeting. We drove some six hours north and west out of Miami, past the Cork Screw Swamp, up beyond Tampa to a cow pasture in a place called Inverness. The usual clearing, the usual platform and row of chairs for robed "dignitaries," the huge wooden cross, and set in a deep purple sky, a yellow, postalcard moon.

"God stamped ugliness on the face of the Jew for the same reason he put rattlers on a snake." Cheers and whoops, and from the audience seated in their automobiles, appreciative horn honking.

"Nigger, he black on the outside, white on the inside. Jew, he white on the outside, black on the inside." More cheers, more whoops, more horn honking.

After it was all over we joined our car to a line that snaked across the pasture, onto a state road, and drove south toward Tampa. Shortly one of those ubiquitous roadside signs, EATS, appeared, and we broke file, as did several other cars, for a coffee break.

Inside my companion and I sat down facing each other on the wall side of a table for four. In no time, two Klansmen sat down alongside of us, facing each other, and for all appearances, we were a congenial foursome. The waitress came along. "What'll you have?" We all ordered coffee.

My friend and I talked artificially about the distance to Tampa; our companions about the "speaking" they had just attended. When the coffee arrived the man at my side turned to me, his leather-tanned outdoor face in friendly repose. "Would you pass the sugar, friend?"

"Sure," and smiling back, I did.

"Thank you."

"You're welcome."

I thought of an hour ago, the calumnies of Jews, the brutish and primitive whoops and hollers they evoked; and here we were pleasing, thank youing, and you're welcoming each other.

Of course, the Klansman didn't know that I was Jewish, but on another similar occasion in a courthouse in Miami with an American Nazi Party member we found ourselves arriving at the same door at the same time. He knew me and I knew him. We both stopped to let each other in, not in mock courtesy but in reflex reaction politeness. He held the door for me and automatically I said "Thank you," and he, "You're welcome."

Interesting, that chivalry in America is associated with the South, in Asia, politeness with Japanese, and in Europe with the Germans. Sadism, too.

The Quality of Our Mercy

Wouldn't it bug you too? I unwind my own litany. Who's talking about the Black Panthers?

My friend is a militant radical. He's also brilliant and perverse. He was explaining and justifying acts of racial violence. "You must bear in mind," he admonished me, "these people have been locked into poverty for generations, as if it were an inheritance or a curse or something, while on their TV sets the good life is sung and for all they know, lived by everyone but themselves. Wouldn't it bug you too? Hungry, poor, they're without any education that's worth a damn, just like their fathers and mothers were before them, and they know damn well that their own kids, no matter the crap from the Urban Coalition, are also going to be functional dummies. Add the frustration of political powerlessness and economic powerlessness . . ."

I interrupted him, and unwound my own litany, i.e., that a society that tolerates violence is a society headed for anarchy, and besides the Negro isn't the world's first poverty-ridden, inadequately educated and powerless human, and what's more, even today he doesn't have an exclusive on these conditions, and if every group with a legitimate bitch emulated the Black Panthers . . .

"Who's talking about the Black Panthers? I was talking about the mountain boys in the North Carolina Ku Klux Klan."

On other occasions he has said much the same thing while justifying the Panthers. The charm that distinguishes him from the current crop of sentimental radicals lies in the fact that his mercilessness is not strained. He's for the misbegotten engaging in guerrilla warfare regardless of their race, color or creed.

But the point of this entry is not my friend.

He had described several objective conditions, i.e., poverty, lack of education, powerlessness, and I, Pavlovian, word-associated black. Most of you reading his interrupted statement did too, despite the same conditions applying equally to the rank and file of the Ku Klux Klan. So my point is us.

We have been far less equivocal about Mississippi violence than about ghetto violence, and the failing lies in our hypocrisy. Because Mississippi is distant we see clearly brutish men victimizing innocent men. Being sane people we hold them morally accountable. In the nearby black slums, an altogether different stimulus to our guilt and on our haplessness, we complicatedly see not men, but "blacks," not lynching, but "acting out their anguish," not on men but on other "blacks" or "whites," and we transform both brute and brutalized from the he or she of them, into sociological types. It's as if they were, unlike Klansmen, non-people and consequently, unlike Klansmen, not morally responsible. So it is that white thugs are depraved and black ones are deprived.

The Revolution and the Craps Shooter

I had the necessary distance. We went to shoot craps. Jekyll and Hyde, double occupancy on the American Plan. It all figured.

We enjoyed Havana before Castro. Even its squalor had charm. Other people's squalor can be that way. The Casbah for instance, and New York's lower East Side, crowded form and color kaleidoscopically, moving, rushing, turning. Or somnolent, dying mountain villages in Italy, their clay colored man-shelters perched precariously on brooding God mountains, vulnerable in vast God scowling skies. Exotic decay, romantic dirt. Social distance is the peep-hole before which the charm turns on, and I had the necessary distance.

But back to Cuba. When Castro came charging out of the hills, I was pleased. Batista was a reactionary dictator and Fidel, hirsute and khaki armored, a socialist Galahad. When the won revolution was a month or so old, a friend and I flew over from Palm Beach. We went to shoot craps, loll in the sun, and to "see the revolution," in just about that order.

I don't remember how I made out at the tables, but very much remember that I liked the revolution. The people's reactions to their Fidel is what did it. They spoke freely now; they hadn't used to. Even the soldiers were impressive. Not for their being victors, nor for so many of them being green teenagers, but because they were the only rifle shouldered soldiers I had ever seen who fit the word "gentle."

We stayed several days, savoring the dice, the sun, and the social significance of it all. Left dilettante, Jekyll and sensuous Hyde, double occupancy on the American Plan.

When our weekend and our stay was winding down I took a final walk in the Hilton area. It was that walk that provided the hint that maybe all that had happened was merely a changing of the guard. For on that day, the revolution figuratively minutes secured, a dozen vendors suddenly materialized on a handful of streets. All hawked the same item, hundreds of machine made busts of Fidel.

The later reversion of Havanans to talking guardedly, the suspension of freedoms, the political arrests, the Red in all of the political nooks and crannies where they had been Black, all figured. It was code written on those graven images. Even a craps shooter could understand it.

Blacks: Underdogs, Overdogs

*We saw Billy Budd with a Communist couple.
Such a Negro! My wife lets go a boo-boo. More
mind remembered than heart felt. My visceral
response to blacks.*

In the early 1950's we saw Billy Budd with a Communist
couple we knew. It was a Wayne University production
featuring a Negro student in a lead role. But such a Negro!
He was so deeply, darkly complected that he suggested
charcoal. This, plus the fact that he was playing an 18th
century British naval officer, prompted my wife's inter-
mission conversation opener: "Isn't that interesting, casting a Negro in that role."

The ensuing silence sounded and felt like plop. Then,
tartly, but in a voice not yet prepared to break off diplomatic relations, the she-Communist answered: "Really, I
didn't notice his race."

We had been sitting front row, center.

In those days, when racial enlightenment shone port-
side, it was *de rigueur* to not notice the differences in race.
My wife, alas, had let go a boo-boo more socially compromising than passing wind. Today, fashion having fickled
our race values, my wife's 20-20 vision of the youth's blackness has become a hip "sensitivity," while our friends of
yore, for having been color blind, are *ex post facto,* "functional racists."

91

For their times, however, both liberal styles, yester-year's mini-seeing of Negro-ness, and today's maxi-seeing of blackness, are sensible.

What I mean is this:

When color was a civil liability, let alone socially leprous, color blind whites served some Negroes to hurdle discrimination, and to a chance at self realization. Color blindness was a humane attitude, largely held and pros-elytized by the white Left. When during the Johnson ad-ministration racism's pall began lifting, color blindness was quickly relegated to the status of horse and buggy race relations. It was now necessary to see the blackness of the Negro, so that we could more responsively minister to those of his black class and black culture wounds that were beyond the medications of color blind civil rights laws. The white Left accommodated itself, albeit in this phase of the accelerating race evolution, Negroes led the way. I'm sure that my Billy Budd friends made the transi-tion but equally sure that being politically programmed, they are still punching out rote answers to questions the critical nuances of which they hear deafly.

There's another interesting reversal that has taken place in the white Left's relation to the Negro. In the days of Jim Crow laws in the South and fallow-lying civil rights laws in the North, the human beingness of a Negro smoth-ered and smoldered in the tight brown bag that was his skin. To white society, the liberal Left excepted, only the skin bag was visible, and all the bags looking alike, Ne-groes as varied human beings were, indeed, Invisible Men. Now that Jim Crow is in retreat, and long dormant civil rights laws have been sown and activated, and it is fash-ionable to see the black forest rather than its trees, there is the danger that we may again lose sight of the Negro as a person, relegate him once more to the status, Invisible

Man. This time, however, not out of a racist perspective, but from a field of vision in which saintliness and sinnerdom are invisible, and the seen blackness of the sinner is as irrationally his acquittal as it is to racists the saint's sentence.

But it's my visceral responses to blacks that I want to get to, the foregoing, my black cerebrations intended only as prologue. The Negro as victim spurred my sense of fraternity, my politics of egalitarianism. That sense and those politics remain with me, but they are more mind remembered than heart felt.

The whys are complex. Black panelists, press-release black rhetoricians, their wrath indiscriminate, their vengeance blind, spray the white liberal Jewishness of me in spittle. Black toughs, in their fighting corners black academic managers who massage their anger, are ambushing firemen, slaughtering policemen, becoming what racists all along warned they were. Anti-Semitism, spoken, orated, written, put-on, and politicized, and Negroes who know better cowardly silent, expediently silent, ungratefully silent.

Hillel: *If I am only for myself, what am I?*, and so my cerebral self sees still the Negro as underdog. Hillel, still: *If I am not for myself, who am I?*, and so my visceral self sees the black too, but as overdog.

We Need Score Cards for Good Guys and Bad Guys

White Is Beautiful. Young Mr. Clean, defendant. Life imitates fiction. Bonnie and Clyde disfocused. A guitar picker and singer. "How many here from Harvard?" I was laughing too. I forget.

In the late 1950's and early 1960's an outbreak of synagogue bombings swept through the South. Those were the years when the Ku Klux Klan and several White Citizens Councils were reviling Jews as the puppeteers of the civil rights movement. (The Councils were formed to wrest social and political power from The State and to bring about decentralized community control. They were premature exponents of Power to the People, believing, however, that White Is Beautiful.)

Finally, in 1962 arrests were made in Florida resulting in a sensational "bombing trial." The protagonists in the case were two young men. One was raised in Nazi Germany and during World War II had been a member of the Hitler Youth. The other was a United States Navy veteran, tall, rangy, fair, he might have been on leave from a recruitment poster.

The Hitler Youth alumnus, a police undercover agent,

was the State's star witness. Young Mr. Clean was the defendant. He was found guilty.

I was peripherally involved in the investigations of the bombings and later, after the trial, when I wrote an article about it, I savored the anomaly of the trial's anti-type casting, the *Achtunger*! who risks his life spying on anti-Semites, vs the nice kid who delivered your newspapers and always called you Sir, and yet, etc.

In those days the anomaly in casting was an oddity, the stuff of fiction. Not today. Life has a way of imitating fiction, and anti-type casting has become so common that yesterday's Anti-Types have become today's Types. I mean, how long ago was it? a year? two? three? when the word "bomber" conjured an image of a sadist-eyed, bourbon-breathed Klansman? And with cause. Today, say "bomber," and the reflex image it conjures is of an educated, nice familied college student. And with cause. For instance, that bombed out New York town house, its cast of characters from Bryn Mawr, Swarthmore, Columbia, last previous residences suggesting the antithesis of red neck country. Indeed, as I write this, the nine children of a shot in the back Boston policeman are newly orphaned. The suspects? One-time students of prestigious New England universities. Banks are bombed and are held up, and our yesterday's images of Bonnie and Clyde grow disfocused, double exposed by Bonnies with a "social conscience" and Clydes consumed not with the Big Heist, but with financing revolution.

Back then, in the early 60's when our imaged enemies looked like movie Bad Guys, our alarm, our indignation, our resolute support of law and its underpinning of an orderly society, were unequivocal. Now our images of sneak bombers and fanatic murderers have changed. They are of our friends' children, and our responses to violence, grown as expansive as a Mississippi Governor's, include, "On the other hand . . ." In 1960 liberal, and indeed, moderate editors and academicians did not importune America to "listen" to the underprivileged, exploited Southern whites, or to the bully undergraduates who were resisting desegregation at Ol' Miss. They didn't then murmur, "They're trying to tell us something." Was their yesteryear's abhorrence of violence, and is their currently more detached view of it, not so much responsive to the *act* of violence as to its declared rationale?

Someone I know was with a North Carolina Klansman when they heard on the radio that Martin Luther King had been assassinated. The Klansman's reaction was, "Hell, niggers ain't assassinated! They're *killed*." And so with many liberals. Their view of political murder is bifurcated. When the victims are blacks or students, and the killers are our old images of reactionaries, the murder is "heinous" and "wanton." When the victims are policemen or merchants, and the killers are our new images of "idealistic" students or of "oppressed" blacks, the "regrettable" murder calls for "greater understanding of the root causes."

My own stereotypes of Bad Guys and Good Guys are in flux too, and recently they confused, no, confounded me. My wife and I attended a country music "Shower of Stars." The featured entertainer was Merle Haggard, a guitar picker and singer whose songs recall the hardships and the satisfactions, somewhat romanticized, of country life. His hits include "I'm an Okie from Muskogee" and "When You're Runnin' Down My Country, Hoss, You're Walkin' on the Fightin' Side of Me." Simplistic songs of patriotism. The audience in the Boston Symphony Hall was "country" and it was poor; you could tell that by the large number of starch dieted overweights, and when they smiled, by their dental work, or their lack of it. They loved Haggard. I did too.

At one point, following a combatively patriotic song, the MC quieted the dinning applause and called out, "How many here from Boston University?" Puzzled silence. "How many here from Brandeis University?" Now the audience was catching on to the joke. Laughter. "How many here from Harvard?" Uproarious laughter. "You uneducated dopes!" Laughter again, superior, smug. Cambridge's unwashed, shoeless Street People, the Boston area's student demonstrators, the murderers of that policeman, all of those college types, were absent presences in Symphony Hall and these unschooled hardworking clerks, laborers, and housewives were laughing at them, and in their laughter congratulating themselves for being gainfully employed, and for loving their country. I was laughing too, and for much the same reasons, when suddenly I felt my wife finger-stabbing me. "What are *you* laughing at!"

It took a moment for me to understand. I had forgotten. I had been asail in Haggard's sounds, I had become one with the audience, they were, I suppose, my Noble Savages, and so I had forgotten that I was vice president of Brandeis University! *I* was *their* image of a Bad Guy!

Fellow-traveling is a precarious pastime.

Of Babylon and Babbitt

*Derbied rich and babushka'd poor, their
arms circling. Beat it Mac, I'm busy. He's
laying in such a funny way. "Drop dead."
I'd hide my wallet under the mattress. The
skull and crossed bones.*

As recently as the 1950's and the early 60's when stage-
crafters and movie makers wanted to suggest the texture
and timbre of New York, they'd musically background a
city vignette with "The Sidewalks of New York." "East
Side, West Side, All Around the Town," *la-de-dum, la-
de-dum*, and sure-fire, the lilting song would conjure a
picture of policemen and tenement dwellers, derbied rich
and babushka'd poor, their arms circling each other's
waist, their comraderie contagious through the silver
screen or across the footlights. Today, it'd be funny. Not
funny, funny. Funny, sad. You can sense it in the person
of the New York cab driver, litmus of the city's tempera-
ment, who has been metamorphosed from garrulous and
good natured kibitzer to suspicious, bayed prey.

When I think of New York and returning to it, I remember the night attendant in a car rental garage who,
when I suggested to him he leave a note for the morning
man telling him that the headlamps on the car I was returning weren't working, responded, "That ain't my job."

I thought to myself to hell with you, and then thinking better, said aloud, "Wait a minute, I'll write it, someone can get killed or something." The man shrugged his shoulders, his expression conveying, Beat it Mac, I'm busy, and he lurched the car forward and away.

Or, New York recalls the cab driver who told my then fifteen year old daughter, "Drop dead." She had come home to our apartment, her hair and summer dress soaked by torrential rains, and toweling her hair, told us there's a taxi downstairs and a man laying in a funny position in the front seat. She was worried for him. He's probably sleeping, I told her. She said, maybe, but he's laying in such a funny way, his motor is on, and the windows are closed.

"If you're that worried, go down and see."

"It's raining so hard."

"Then stop worrying."

She couldn't, and quickly changing into something dry, she left. Five minutes later she was back. She had knocked on the window. The man hadn't stirred. She knocked harder. The man moved, rose partially, turned the window down, and asked her, "Yeah?" He had indeed been asleep and she said, "I'm sorry, I thought maybe you were sick."

"Drop dead," and he went back to sleep.

During the early 1950's I used to travel the Mountain States, stopping in places like Casper and Laramie, Wyoming; Trinidad and La Junta, Colorado; Las Vegas and Roswell, New Mexico. When I'd come into town the evening before my morning meetings, I liked walking the city's downtown and nearby dingy side streets around the bus or railroad station. Before leaving my hotel room, I'd hide my wallet under the mattress, remove my tie and "dress down," fearing, because the streets were not my

streets and its Indian, Mexican and mixed breed faces
not the faces with which I grew up in New York, that
business-suited I would seem wealthy, a target for toughs.
Nothing ever happened. Nothing ever nearly happened.
Today in New York City, I have friends who will not take
nighttime walks no matter the streets are their own, its
faces childhood familiar. I have one friend on the West
Side near Central Park who refuses to be intimidated,
does take after dinner walks, but leaves his wrist watch
home. And the New York parks, Central, Prospect, a doz-
en and more others, with posted signs cautioning strollers
to Stay Out such and such hours, written warnings like
the skull and crossed bones on medicine cabinet labels.

What has happened is that New York City has become what my imagination feared foreign skid rows were.
Trinidad, however, turned out to be innocent, my fear my
own hang up and The Sidewalks of New York, *la-de-dum*,
is where the goblins are alive and well.

Fear, it seems, grows thick where music and art and
theatre thrive, and the streets are safe where Babbitt
lives.

"I Want to Fight Fascism"
(I Told Him)

Downtown at the Marine Corps recruiting station. I didn't want to tell him why. War is getting a bad name. What my neatly hair cutted self had in common with today's shaggy hairs.

The one question I wasn't prepared for was, "Why?" It was 1942, in Washington, D.C., I was going to school there, a freshman at Georgetown University, and I was downtown at the Marine Corps recruiting station, to enlist. "Why?" the sergeant wanted to know, and suddenly I was embarrassed. I had been trying to breathe slower, to will sedation for the excitement that for days had been welling larger and larger in me, and on which I was now afloat. His surprise question drained my excitement and that was good because breathing regularly I felt mature, like I wanted to seem, but it embarrassed me and so again I felt my kiddishness showing, compromising the maturity I was trying to project.

I was embarrassed because I didn't want to tell him why. It seemed too personal an answer, appropriate for late night bull sessions, but inappropriate, even corny, somehow pompous, voiced to a Sigmund Romberg uni-

formed marine I had just met. Finally, my eyes shyer than
my voice, I uttered my private truth.

"I want to fight Fascism."

We had something in common, now. It was the one
answer for which he wasn't prepared.

I have been thinking back to World War II. Likely,
it's my age, reminiscing seems to be a function of it. But
majorly, it's Vietnam and its social and political tribu-
taries, that draws me back to it and to an accompanying,
nagging notion that nowadays war is getting a bad name
and peace, too favorable a press. I am not discussing Vietnam here as either a good or a bad war. What I am saying
is that in the arguments leveled at our Vietnam involve-
ment, war *as such* is getting the bad name. So much so for
instance, that Margaret Mead has described World War
II as ". . . a war that culminated in the horrors of Hiro-
shima." To a point, true. A wiser, more perceptive one,
however, would be that it was a war that culminated in
the closing down of the crematoria, in an end to ongoing
genocide.

World War II was a good war and it wasn't the first
such. More importantly (the resonance I intend in these
grumblings), it must not be the last war, lest all the preceding good ones and their trophies of national and personal freedom are forfeit. Conversely, for all its currently
good press, peace has been known to be bitter. In some
places it still is and unless warred on, life is bitter too.
Great numbers of enlistees, "interventionists" of the
youth generation of the early 1940's, understood that there
can be peace in war, tyranny in peace, and they understood it with no less idealism, no less love of life, than is
lyricized by modern day folk guitarists.

. . . I have paused—stopped is more accurate— in my
typing of these paragraphs. Rereading them, redrafting

them, rereading them again and again redrafting them, I
feel troubled. They do not do my bidding. I have not craft-
ed my words so that they are my thoughts' fine and faith-
ful brushes. Instead I sense that I am their unwittingly
forming portrait, a portrait I don't much like. "Peace in
war" is only a shade of meaning removed—a running
shade—from War Is Beautiful, and resembles me to Dr.
Strangelove. Younger, I laughed nervously at him. Now,
myself, middle aged, is it the inadequacy of my word art,
or something more profound, more disquieting deep within me that suggests the resemblance?

I also detect a narcissism, my middle years' affection
for the reflection of my nineteen years self as I write now
of me then, that I "understood." And crabbiness is there
too, the "folk guitarists" and "lyricizing" language.

Might it be argued that the moral conviction and
physical courage that marked the act of enlistment in
World War II has its counterpart today, in those who re-
fuse to serve? I think the argument makes a case.

But I have a more discomforting thought concerning
the two generations. I remember my feelings of welling
guilt when as a student, not yet in service, I saw a soldier,
or comradely groups of soldiers. I too wanted to be uniformed, to not be a civilian, to feel a part of the soldiering
Group. Whether it was a stronger feeling than wanting to
fight Fascism, I cannot measure now, nor say now which
feeling triggered the bus ride to the enlistment station.
Even in this writing, as I try, without romance, to understand my then self better, I am certain only that I responded to both promptings, and that the desire to belong, to conform, was strong. And so I wonder whether my
conformity, too, has its counterpart in today's draft dodg-
ers. Can it be that as it was the "in" thing to be uniformed then, it is the "in" thing to dodge service today?

And if this is so, did my neatly haircutted self have in common with today's shaggy hairs, not individual bravery, but herd conformity?

I MUST BE GETTING OLDER

Before I begin what I want to say, I want to say something. When I was thirty, nothing, absolutely nothing, made me as aware of the fact that I was no longer twenty as meeting a teacher or a policeman who was younger than myself. Somehow teachers and policemen should have been older than me. Hadn't they always been? Even now, when I meet someone richer, or more accomplished, and yet younger than I am, it reminds me more sharply than even my worsening sacroiliac, that I've peaked the prime of my years. In fact, I sometimes think that if it weren't for the existence of young people, I'd not know I was getting older. And so if I talk about my sideburns here, it's my getting on in years that I'm really talking of, and am glad about. I'm glad because I like coasting, and middle age is just the right sized hill.

But middle age is more than sideburns, whether shaven short in memorial celebration of one's Lost Youth, or grown long in entente cordiale with Youth's current army of occupation. For me it has meant expanded tolerance (because I care less?) and contracting illusions (day dreams I'm afraid have an eleventh hour). I write about these too, albeit my reflections are about commencement exercises and what I want to be when finally I grow up. And something else. If along the way these pages meander, younger readers are puzzled by allusions to such unlikely names as Ginger Rogers, I have anticipated the hurdle such references are to cross generational communication, but am nevertheless standing pat, metaphorically, that is. I'll tell you why.

Recently, a Boston area underground newspaper carried a photograph of President Nixon, doctored to resemble Adolf Hitler. It was done ably. So ably that both Nixon and Hitler were simultaneously recognizable in the single picture. Upon observing to a student that whatever one might think of Richard Nixon, a Hitler he isn't, and continuing, My god, think for a moment all that Hitler represents, the answer I got, was: Come off it, Mr. Perlmutter, and smiling amiably, For all that it matters to us, Hitler might as well be Attila the Hun.

Well, if our young need a refresher course on the Third Reich, explanatory notes about Hollywood and Vine seem a wasted effort. Besides, as people with operations have surgery stories in common, reflections on middle age are really, after all, primarily for middle aged audiences. They'll understand.

Unto Thine Ownself

A talking cornstalk. Understanding Nixon voters. A freckled songstress. That was it!

My shaving my long sideburns that night was an act of protest, and the lather of both can be attributed to Lawrence Welk. Had my chair been less deep and less comfortable, I'd have changed the channel. But it wasn't and now, here he was in my livingroom, "uh-one," "uh-two," by God, a talking cornstalk. I recall thinking a smile, a patronizing one of course, and thinking too, let him be, watch him awhile, you'll better understand those *Reader's Digest* subscribers who voted Nixon.

He played an old Jimmy Dorsey number in the Jimmy Dorsey style. I remembered it; he played it well. Next came Clyde McCoy's "Sugar Blues," trembling trombone, the works; it was good. He recreated the swing and the blues of the Thirties and early Forties, and as warmly and appealingly as a serendipitously found old photograph album. His music wafted me back to my youth. Finally a Tommy Dorsey favorite—three vocalists, two crew-cut All-America types, and a pretty pert-nosed and freckled songstress. That was it! I rose, strode into the bathroom and in a declaration of comradeship with my own generation and its style, I shaved an inch from my sideburns, thereby saying no! to creeping hippieism.

111

World War II Was a B Movie

Whatever was phony. Dialogue. Your generation hasn't suffered what we have. John Wayne.

Recently, in San Francisco, I saw a Ruby Keeler double feature, both parts of which dated back to the Thirties. In one, forgettably titled, she played opposite Al Jolson; the second feature was something called *Flirtation Walk* with Dick Powell as a boyish West Point cadet. When the movie let out and the lights went on I noted that I was probably the oldest of several dozen viewers. It didn't surprise me. Throughout the two movies, where I merely smiled my derision, the audience greeted Busby Berkeley pretensions, ingenue posturings and you-mixed-up-little-fool-I-love-you lines, with delighted guffaws and good-natured oh-God-no! protests. Their game—and it was fair—was whatever was phony, and the scripts were well-stocked preserves.

Several weeks later I was among young people again. By young people, I mean late teens and early twenties. This time the context was political and rather than being joined in an audience, we were engaged in conversation, or "dialogue" as they preferred to call it. At one point of ruptured frustration, a young man of learning and sensitivity desperately shot at me, "You wouldn't understand. Your generation hasn't suffered what we have. Yours was easy!" I might more effectively have pleaded the Fifth, but instead testified briefly to the Depression and to World War II. It was to no avail. The complicated reasons aside, I think it was partly because World War II, to the under-thirties, is really an old John Wayne movie on the Late Show, or it's both parts of a campy double feature, so badly done the subject is trivial. Besides, can anyone imagine John Wayne *suffering*?

World War III Is a Home Movie

The chairman of the board and the valedictorian.
The old man was about forty. The boy murdered
his mother. Perhaps it's just as well.

Last June I attended a commencement exercise at which a
sizable number of the graduating students wore, over their
gowns, sheets with stenciled red fists, the symbol of violent revolution. Both the chairman of the board of trustees
and the valedictorian might have been sent by central
casting. Their scripts too were predictable. The chairman, the kind who addressed you-people-out-there, re-
counted the reforms the university had made, allowed as
how there was still a job to be done, suggested the wisdom
of patience, etc. Parents applauded heartily. It was now
the valedictorian's turn. Where the chairman was sure in
his manner, the valedictorian was in his virtue; where the
older man patronized his audience, the younger man lec-
tured it. He prosecuted the university, flayed adults,
scorned the professed values of the parents. If the students' applause was a thermometer, their contempt for
mom and dad ran high. From mom and dad's section of
the amphitheater, applause was scattered, thinly.

After the ceremonies, among the many chatting
groups of students, parents and faculty, I marked one in
particular. It was a short, overdressed woman, standing

on tiptoes, puckering a kiss for planting on her tall son's cheek. The boy was one of the students who had chosen to wear the blood red fist. In seconds he would perfunctorily bend to accommodate her, but at that moment he had not yet decided he would. His henna-haired mama, fairly aglow with pride, mercifully did not note (I'd like to think) the boy's expression of impatient hostility.

The vignette reminded me of two stories, one, from Columbia University by way of a reporter, and the other from the ghetto—the one in Poland—by way of my mother's storytelling.

First, Columbia. On campus during the SDS take-over and police bust of 1968 a young combatant, spotting an adult passerby, screamed at him, "Die, old man, die!" The "old man" was about forty. There was no indication that he was on one side or the other, or that he was an administrator, professor, reporter, or anything or anybody in particular. He was, however, clearly, an adult and so, "Die, old man, die!" . . .

My mother's story is of the youth to whom the devil offered the satisfaction of any wish he might make, the sole condition being the boy's delivering his mother's heart. Propelled by fantasies of sublime gratification, the boy hurried home, murdered his mother, cut her heart out, placed it on a tray, and then ran to present it to the devil. On the way he stumbled and fell and his mother's heart rolled into the street. As he reached for it to continue with it to his tryst, the heart spoke. Softly it said: "Did you hurt yourself, my son?"

There is a tension between the generations that exceeds those of the last several generations of parents and their young adult children. Indeed, on some fronts the generational tension has flared, as skirmishes do between nations. Perhaps it's just as well for the future of our species that in our generational war, albeit the enemy is adrenalized by youth, our side is sedated by parenthood.

When I Grow Up

*A windowed sign saying ROOMS. I
was wakened by a godawful sound. A
con-man if ever I saw one. A centenarian songbird. A hangman has satisfactions.*

I was scouting Washington, D. C.'s DuPont Circle area
because a room there would give me convenient transpor-
tation to both my night job at the War Department and
my day classes at Georgetown's Foreign Service School,
and sure enough there it was, a nice brownstone and a windowed sign saying ROOMS. A long minute after I had
rung the door bell atop the tall stoop, a gaunt, grey and
bent woman of perhaps seventy-five opened the door,
focused me in her weak eyes, and asked me, Yes? Perhaps too loudly—I assumed she was hard of hearing—I
helloed her and told her I was interested in her ROOMS
sign, and did she have one. I'm a student at Georgetown,
I added, thinking she might be Irish. She invited me in
and turning from me, walked to the stairs and cocking
her head upwards, shouted to the next landing, "Mother!
Mother! Come down."

Her mother—I forget their names—for all that she
must have been in her mid-nineties, looked two hundred.
They were good enough landladies, odd, but nice, but

what I want to tell about them—the mother, really—is this. In my first Sunday of tenancy, I was wakened by a godawful sound that made me think of a dog in piteous pain. If you listened closely as in my puzzlement I did, the dog seemed to be running over piano keys. I scampered from my bed, pulled trousers over my undershorts, grabbed a shirt and rushed downstairs to see what was happening.

I saw it and didn't believe it. There in the living room standing tall and erect by the piano was mother, belting out an aria. Seated at the piano was a waxed haired, waxed moustachioed accompanist, a con-man if ever I saw one.

The scene was replayed for all of the Sundays of my tenancy there. The man's name was Alfonse or maybe it was Antonio, and he was a voice teacher and wouldn't you guess, mother and daughter called him Maestro. Mother, it turned out, was practicing for her debut in Constitution Hall. The maestro was certain, or so he told even me, that she had a rare and exquisitely beautiful voice and that soon, soon, he would have it readied for the world. Following each Sunday's practice session, daughter would serve tea, we'd talk inanities, the great voices he had trained in Italy, the acoustics at La Scala, and soon he'd rise, the signal for daughter to place several bills in his long fingered hand, and looking charming all the while, he would take leave. Several months later when I moved, the scene was still being played.

I'll return to the maestro and his centenarian songbird in a moment, but want now to talk of myself. I am a vice president of a distinguished university. My primary responsibility is to raise money for the funding of the school's budget. In short, my title is a euphemism for fundraiser.

Now who among us as a child wanted to grow up to be a fundraiser? A fireman, yes, a cowboy, yes, a doctor, a lawyer, even a Robin Hood, but a fundraiser? a CPA? A realtor? Such ambitions in a child would properly frighten a parent. But here I am, a grown man, a fundraiser.

To be sure, there are satisfactions in being a fundraiser, or an accountant, or a corporate executive, or "being in soft goods," or maybe hard goods, but I suppose even a hangman gets some satisfaction from doing his job well. The point is, the point remains, that most of us spend our lives doing things we never dreamed we would, and we do it day in, day out, all the while deepening our rut while the light at the end of the tunnel grows dimmer.

We have a private, funny-sad expression in our home. Sometimes I'll say to my wife, When I grow up, I'm going to be a forest ranger.

Which takes me back to the bizarre goings on in that house on DuPont Circle. That so skinny, so wrinkled, scraggly grey and balding ancient canary isn't nearly so ludicrous in my memory now grown thirty years wiser, as she seemed to me at nineteen. After all, undaunted, she was still striving toward the goal she set for herself, and still planning to grow up, she was still young, younger than my fundraiser self has often felt. And larcenous Alfonse? Come to think of it, he was not really such a bad guy, not really.

Sex Isn't What It Used to Be

*My father sold condoms. He is an accessory be-
fore the fact. I am in the cellar with Frankie and
Annie. "You wanna see us fuck?" A different
kettle of fish. No more lying. Natural sex.*

I don't remember how old I was, maybe eleven, maybe
twelve, but old enough to know what condoms were when
I discovered that my father sold them. It was late one
night, I had left my bed for whatever reason, entered the
lit kitchen, and there on our table were the contents of
my father's brown metal suitcase. My father was a peddler, the suitcase his general store. Nights, he would in-
ventory the stock left over from his day's door to door
sales. On this particular night he had left his spread of
razor blades and combs, toothpastes and styptic sticks,
and apparently gone downstairs for a walk. The familiar
Gillettes and Colgates were all there, but something else
too that I had not seen on the table before. My eyes fell—
literally, for what I saw stumbled my reaction—on the
condoms. Pop sold scumbags! I felt shamed. For him, for
myself. It wasn't simply that I hadn't associated sex—our
word was "screwing"—with adults, and certainly not with
my own father—but that sex was somehow *unlofty*, not a
respectable adult's activity, and while I secretly envied
the boys who boasted its experience, I thought it sinful.

And now, alas, my own father was an accessory before the fact.

I don't know where I developed this sense of sex as forbidden. Certainly not in my home. The subject was never once discussed there. In the "streets" is too easy an explanation, and for myself at least, I know that I considered "screwing" as being somehow "bad" long before the days of my corner drug store education. In fact, one of my earliest recollections is of the time when I was five years old and I was in the cellar with Frankie and Annie, the janitor's children, a year and two older than myself. I had been playing in our tenement's yard, had wandered into the cellar, and hearing my name whispered saw them near the boiler. Hi, I said.

"You wanna see us fuck?" Frankie. Conspiratorially.

I had no idea what it meant, but the whispered nature of the invitation, the clandestine setting, suggested something forbidden. "Watch," and so saying, Frankie dropped his knee pants while his sister stepped out of her panties. Barebottomed, they stood facing each other, their children's bodies touching. Nothing more. And as if to edify me, Frankie turned his head to me and said, "We're fucking." I was taken with what I saw and Frankie sensing it, offered, "You wanna get behind Annie? We'll both fuck."

This, however, frightened me. Standing in front of Annie, while naughty, nonetheless seemed nice, but the prospect of standing behind her was a different kettle of fish. I suddenly wheeled and bolted out the cellar door.

Not a word of what I had seen or heard did I tell my mother. I didn't tell her because somehow I knew that I had experienced something forbidden. This, despite my having had absolutely no previous knowledge or awareness of sex.

In all of my growing up years, sex was something lied about, something stolen, and something very, very private. It was lied about because to confess to not having experienced it while in the company of those who boasted it, somehow suggested that you were retarded. So you lied and thereby certified your manliness. Stolen, because it was something girls had and presumably guarded. To get it, boys required a "good line," i.e., the ability to con a girl into acquiescence. So you conned. And it was private. From my behind closed doors readings in *Spicy Magazine* to petting in darkened movie houses and on benches after nightfall on the Williamsburg Bridge, sex was savored privately. How else eat forbidden fruit? While maintaining dignity, that is.

Then one day you fall in love. With or without marriage, sex, only yesterday sinful, is now holy. No more lying; a sharp drop in conning; privacy, however, remains a constant. What I mean to say is that our sex, whether pursued as sin or expressed as love, if it is nothing else, is a private affair. As sin because our transgressions are no one else's business; as love because privacy heightens tenderness. I suppose it's because to sin, as well as to love, is human.

Today, however, sex seems to have gone public. Sexploitation films are a substantial share of the movie industry's output. Theatres specializing in these films, only yesterday confined to sleezy downtown areas, are sprouting in residential neighborhoods. Corner drug stores feature as regular book rack fare hard core pornography. "Live sex" is boldly advertised in New York. And if this form of vicarious sex is for the middle aged consumer, the real thing, *sans* hang ups, *sans* fees, *sans* fears of pregnancy, for pairs and for groups, has become part of the so-called Youth Culture. No longer "forbidden," no longer "sinful," now "natural," sex is no longer private. We have become as liberated as fornicating dogs, while Frankie and Annie, back there in the cellar, whispering and hiding, are in retrospect two modest kids.

And something else. All the while that we have been shedding the privacy which distinguished our sex from Fido's, our young men have been growing longer hair, wearing clothes fashioned by women's clothing designers, and our young women are a major market for Levi's.

It's almost as if sex having gone public, the sexes needed to be camouflaged.

The Poor and the Privileged

Mama sold ices. As if from a monkey, I became a man. How I considered Notary Publics. My rich familied friends.

We were on relief in the 1930's and while my father was still with us, he worked a shovel for the WPA. My mother was the only woman in the neighborhood who sold ices in the streets. She did it from behind a pushcart that weighed several times her ninety pounds. That embarrassed me. Not the relief so much, or the WPA, but that my mother sold ices. Even the gentile women in the near-by neighborhoods, some of whom we knew drank beer, didn't do man's work.

Several times in my adult life I've had occasion to say that we had been on relief, had been on the receiving line of government issued flour, sugar, shirts, sweaters and the like. I've said it to friends to make some point about poverty, but usually they hear it as a pitiable description of what it means to be underprivileged, and their eyes gloss with admiration for me, as if from a monkey I became a man, so I'm careful of saying it any more.

Poor, we surely were. I thought my Aunt Esther was rich because she and my Uncle Max had a stuffed chair. More than poor, we were innocent. I considered Notary

Publics to be Very Important People, and when I once persuaded one to write a letter of recommendation for me—I was sixteen—I was cloud nined by my whirl with high society. But underprivileged? Had someone suggested it to us, we'd have considered him a case for Bellevue.

My rich familied friends, whom I now spare my childhood's bad times, and their compassionate like, overuse and misapply "underprivileged" to the point where they've drained the term of its meaning. They look at a neighborhood, note the absence of the amenities they themselves have known, and assume that here is emotional or psychological deprivation. I suspect that they think this because were they to experience the loss of their accustomed-to amenities, that's what they would suffer. Natural enough. Ironically, however, it's this middle class, middle brow, liberal community that is Mom and Dad to a substantial proportion of the hippy population. Theirs are the kids who live in primitive communes, who are the illy clad, poorly nourished Street People, the poor not by chance but by choice who, quite plainly, want out. The children of the so-called underprivileged, however, both white and black, want in.

My political self fellow-travels with the various Coalitions striving to depolarize the distance between the rich and the poor. Another part of me, whimsically, because it has been poor and so is knowing, would like to see a committee, replete with a letterhead, a full page *New York Times* advertisement, and a benefit party hosted by Beautiful People, concern itself with the polarization between our privileged selves and our overprivileged children.

Black Kids Remind Me

"We'se talkin' White." Putting on airs.
When I am on the phone with someone I feel
I should impress.

A friend of mine, an elementary school teacher in a Southern city, has an assignment called "Special Education." The term is a euphemism for courses designed to upgrade the reading and writing levels of academically retarded children. Her class is made up of Negro children ranging in age from eight to twelve. She tells the story of how one day she happened along while several of them were laughing from deep in their bellies, and upon seeing her, braked their laughter, but eyeing her affectionately, continued tittering behind mouth covering hands intended, unsuccessfully, to suppress the sounds of their glee. She's a warm person, my friend, and shortly elicited from them what it was that was so funny. She suspected it was herself, and was right. As one of the children explained, "We'se talkin' White." Thereupon, in response to her encouragement, one of them rendered an imitation of their teacher's speech rhythm and word pronunciation. It was a good imitation. Later when the joke waned, the children got back into their old speech shoes, and the class in diction began.

The board of education, no matter its vague course

title, considers the class as one in which correct English is being taught. The children, however, obviously regard it as instruction in "talkin' White." What impressed me about the story, however, was that the children *knew* "correct English," how else ably imitate it? Consequently, in communicating with each other in their own dialect, they were making a conscious choice, and not at all revealing a speech deprivation.

In fact, when I was in Williamsburg, I remember being very conscious of "sissy" talk and "regular" talk. We knew, for instance, the correct pronunciation of such words as "can," "span," "ran," etc., and when grammar school teachers grew finicky, we indulged them by saying it "their way." In the streets, however, we modified the broad "a," enunciating it as in "bare," "rare," etc. To say it teacher's way when we were among ourselves was putting on airs, talking "sissy" talk.

And as to speech rhythms, to this day, when I am on the phone with a stranger, or with someone whom I instinctively feel I should impress, I sometimes am conscious of the rhythm of my voice and am embarrassed that it is pretentious, not really my natural voice, and that I am "talking Gentile."

Perhaps speech patterns are like clothing styles. As I knew as a boy how to correctly pronounce "can" but wouldn't, I could have, had I chosen, worn trousers that were knee length rather than "longies." I didn't because to do so in my milieu would have been embarrassing, a suggestion that I was trying to be "fancy," like the kids in the rich neighborhoods. Even worse, it would have constituted a form of "passing," a desertion of my "gang."

It may just be that those kids in the Special Education class aren't so much retarded as they are loyal to their own.

Sometimes You Have to Learn to be Wrong

We never had a father and son relationship. Walking the Williamsburg Bridge. I lied I didn't feel like one. I resolve as a matter of principle to not enjoy the movie.

My father and mother were separated when I was sixteen, my brother thirteen. Actually, "separated" was a euphemism we used to cover our shame for his having deserted us. One day, about a year after he left, he suddenly appeared to "see the children." We had never had the father and son relationship that I had envied in boys' books, or in Mickey Rooney movies. In fact, we didn't have any social relationship at all. Evenings, after my school and his work, I entered my world, the streets, and he, his, his friends, or he was upstairs, tired. Weekends, the same. Consequently, when he returned to visit, and to pick up with us, there having been no social connection that had been severed, there were no contact points to be soldered. For him, his months-long anticipated visit was a pathetic illusion, and my righteousness—I was my mother's partisan—ground it to delusion.

In any event, we walked the Williamsburg Bridge, he testing conversation openers about school, are you seeing girls, his travels. It was our first "conversation" ever, and it came on stumbling and painful, he doggedly trying, I punitively monosyllabic.

At long last, we reached the bridge's Manhattan side and there were Fred Astaire and Ginger Rogers at the Loew's Delancey Street. Pop suggested we have an ice cream, I lied I didn't feel like one, and he tried again, saying let's go to that movie. He had never taken me to a movie before and it was plain that he was trying hard to be a buddy, like fathers in the Hardy Boys or in the Tom Swifts. Also I understood that the darkness of the theatre, its voices and its music, and our required silence would be respites from my stiffness that he'd welcome.

I acceded saying, okay, good idea, but simultaneously resolved to not enjoy the movie. It wasn't that I, too, didn't welcome Fred Astaire making the two of us a crowd, not at all. Rather my resolve to not enjoy the movie was a matter of principle. I wouldn't let my deserter-father, by buying me in, buy me out.

Today I'm not as up-tight about my virtue, am far more open to a deal than I was at the Loew's Delancey. That goes for my relationship with my father, with my son, and for that matter, with City Hall, and Washington, D. C. What I mean is, when you are young and *know* you are right, you haven't yet learned that it's sometimes wrong to be right.

A FAMILY ALBUM

Before I begin what I want to say, I want to say something. Born in the Twenties and now the father of grown children, I am of a generation that has been sandwiched between foreign born parents and children who are foreigners to us. When I was a grade schooler and Miss Harrington or Miss Dawson or whichever of the greying Irish Misses who were our teachers, having had it with my misbehavior, asked to see my mother, I was embarrassed. Not because I misbehaved, but because my mother had an accent. More precisely—because it's what really mattered to me—a Jewish accent. I secretly wished that my mother would seem less Jewish, more worldly. Today, myself grown more Jewish with age, listening to my children, I try to hear in them an echo of my mother's accent. Its faintness saddens me. I would have them be less worldly, more Jewish.

My first New York City address was on the lower East Side. My last, on the upper East Side. Then we were poor, relief poor. Now an accountant does my income tax. Our generation outgrew bad times like they were boys' shirts or pimples. It seemed natural to suffer them and natural to outgrow them. But here too, irony has set in. We're uptown today, or in Westchester, or on Long Island, and the only poor with whom we relate are our aging parents—or our coming-of-age children. As we ran from poverty, leaving our parents behind downtown, so now are our children turning from our affluence, leaving us behind, uptown.

But I am getting too serious and mean only to be reflective. In these pages I write of my mother and my aunt, my uncle and my father-in-law, and how I remember them in times when they were younger than I am now, and I write of our todays too, when three of them are freshly dead, and one is very tired. I am here too, tom-peeping my boyhood from behind years that are gradually piling higher.

Mama

Mom was the only Anglo. The stones know me here. Half empty Coca Cola bottles. We came out onto the street.

2-C is a clean, three-room railroad flat in a dirty Brooklyn tenement house. After 42 years of living in it, my mother has moved in with my aunt on Coney Island. Her former neighborhood was once all-Jewish. It is now overwhelmingly Puerto Rican and Negro, and with Mom's departure, the building is all Puerto Rican and Negro. I used to tease her, wanting her to move, that she was the "only Anglo" left in the building. (Compared with my mother's, Molly Goldberg's accent sounds like Julie Andrews'.)

But she wouldn't. As she put it, "the stones know me here." Also, up and down the street, there were her friends, a thinning assortment of elderly Jewish widows. Importantly too, 2-C was the place to which she could always return following stays with us. In a sense that I understood well, it was her sure refuge from dependency on "the children." It was her turf; it represented her independence.

In the past year, however, the window-barred apartment was broken into twice. Her valuables, consisting of several sheets, pillow cases and a blanket, were stolen.

137

Also stolen were the contents of her small refrigerator, including half empty Coca Cola bottles. Mom, though she minimized it, "It's time already," was frightened. Then my uncle died and my aunt, her sister, was alone too. Now they live together in an apartment house with an elevator on Coney Island.

It's the moving from 2-C, however, that I want to write about.

Forty-two years is a long time. From that apartment my brother and I walked off to kindergarten, to war, to the marriage altar. On the day of moving it was Mom, who had been always waiting, who was at last walking out. In the center of the bare-walled middle room stood several cord-tied grocery and drugstore cardboard boxes containing miscellaneous dishes and pots, pictures, and a motley assortment of broken toys and tattered dolls long discarded and forgotten by her grandchildren.

The fewness and the raggedyness of the cartons seemed to mock the meaning of her life. Was that all it took to wrap up 42 years?

As we left, I tried to etch the scene in my memory, but surreptitiously so as to minimize the occasion. We walked down the stairs, past doors and landings that were familiar, but whose occupants were strangers, and came out onto the street. There, by the stoop, in symbolism any self-respecting fiction editor would reject, lay a dead rat.

I later had a second thought about it. "At least," I thought, "it was dead."

Tanta Ida

*He came unannounced. They are
each of them waiting. What are
we? Fancy ladies? She died sitting upright. My introduction to
chow mein. The American ambassador. A rabbi, a stranger.
The nature of loneliness.*

I'm at that age now, 47, when death visits the family more
and more often. We knew he was coming for Uncle Willie.
He came unannounced for *Tanta* Ida. The long distance
telephone call, the drive from Boston to Brooklyn, Who'd
Have Thought Last Night We'd Be Driving to New York
This Morning?, the cemetery gatherings with long unvisi-
ted cousins and uncles and aunts. Four times this year,
and it's scattering and confusing my memory. The childhood formed memory of my family's faces is slipping from
me, and my driving-back-to-Boston new forming memories of them are of greying faces, mourning eyed and
mourning voiced. For long years our family has been dis-
persed, in Miami, in Chicago, in Boston, and now death
has drawn us close again, and our remaining uncles and
aunts have newly in common their diminishing fewness
and that they are each of them waiting.

My *Tanta's* death stunned us, she hadn't been ill,

and on actuarial charts there were years, more than a few, left her. Still, we should have known and I think maybe I did. Two months earlier, returning from the cemetery unveiling of my Uncle Willie's tombstone—Willie was *Tanta's* husband—I suggested to *Tanta* and to my mother, Let's all go to Israel this summer. For years I had been suggesting they go to Florida during the winter and always the answer was, Maybe next year. What that really meant was, Nathan, don't be foolish, what will old women like us do in Miami? What are we? Fancy ladies? We belong here and we're comfortable here. "Here" in recent years was Coney Island, before that, Williamsburg. But this time, as if they had anticipated my suggestion and had discussed it beforehand, first *Tanta* and then my mother said, Yes, they'd like to see Israel. The thought flickered on my mind that this was their way of acknowledging death's nearness, of saying, Yes, before we die we really should see Israel. I hurried the thought away, but I think I was right, that *Tanta* knew.

She died sitting upright on the couch in front of the television set. It was nighttime, my mother already asleep, awoke, and the living room lights and television voices on, she began scolding *Tanta*, Foolish woman, do you think Perry Mason's feelings will be hurt if you go to sleep?, and following her scolds into the living room, she found her sister dead.

By noon of that day we had all of us converged on the funeral parlor, and my aunt too, in a handsome mahogany box. Contemplating her in the coffin, a smiling thought occurred to me. For all that it had been fully half a century since as a girl she came to America, had you yesterday heard her accent, seen her wardrobe, talked with her a little, you'd have known what any New York passerby would have casually assumed. That that woman you hear

talking, or that woman who just passed by, or even now,
the woman dead in the box, is, a little, old, Jewish lady.
And why I smiled is that when I was a preschool boy,
Tanta, several years my mother's junior and then childless, was my concept of Being American! Alone among
the female adults I knew, *Tanta* it was who could read to
me in English (how was I to know at four or five that it
was decidedly less than King's English?); who took me to
the movies; who taught me to play solitaire; and who introduced me to chow mein. Our kitchen, which served
both as our living room and our play room, our street, our
father and mother were all part of our day-in, day-out
world, a somehow Jewish world; but childless *Tanta* and
a game of cards, *Tanta* reading me the Sunday comics,
Tanta and eating chow mein were the outside world,
America. I smiled at her death's mask, What a nice American ambassador you were, *Tanta.*

Later that day in the cemetery by the drizzle-moist,
earth-brown excavation next to Uncle Willie's still shiny
new tombstone, a rabbi, a stranger, spoke to us, her inti-
mates, about *Tanta's* life. Ready-to-wear generalities,
Loving Mother, Devoted Wife, Daughter of Israel, clichés
designed to hang loosely on whichever *Tanta* might have
died today, or will tomorrow. Two months earlier, mourning grouped two feet to the right of where we now huddled,
another rabbi, another stranger, similarly glibly eulo-
gized Uncle Willie's life. Then, and now again, my younger cousins bristled. They resented the canned eulogy, its
oversized clichés clashed with their tightly worn grief. It
was as if they felt, Surely, in this moment of burial, in
this moment preceding eternal interment, a pause for
authentic feeling, even a small one, is at last due Life.

My uncles and aunts and my mother too, however,
didn't notice, let alone mind. I noticed and I didn't mind.

Perhaps because my uncles and aunts, longer-lived than my cousins, are less romantic about Life. Perhaps too, the older among us knew *Tanta*, and the eulogizer could neither add nor detract from our lived through memories of her, our privately possessed life remainder in her. Also, the funeral is a religious rite whose race remembered form, rather than its personal conceits, confirms our having lived and died as Jews. And a traditional rabbi, even a stranger, is preferable to a layman, even an intimate, else the public funeral is for a lonely runner's death rather than for a mother's daughter, herself a son's mother, a relay runner in Israel.

Now my mother is alone. Her peers are gone. No matter there are grandchildren; they are grown and self reliant, and so it's the absence of peers that makes for loneliness, and that I want to comment on now.

On the way back from the cemetery, en route to the apartment my mother and aunt shared, a long time family friend made a silly remark, so characteristically silly, we all, Mama included, smiled. Later, in the apartment, my mother mused, If Ida were alive, I'd be gossiping with her now about what Avraham said. With whom will I gossip foolishness now?

Who indeed? Isn't it an astounding mathematical phenomenon that in this world populated by three billion, five hundred million people, there are men and women for whom there is no one, not a one, with whom to be comfortably foolish?

I, Gangster

I am part of a Theft Ring. It was a matter of principle. My destination is disaster. I play my trump card.

I was eleven, maybe twelve years old when I discovered There Are Some Things Money Can't Buy. My pal, Cockeye Georgie, and I led after-school lives as a Book and Magazine Theft Ring. We stole only such books and magazines as we intended reading and, once read, we sold them to second-hand bookstores. Those we couldn't sell or for which we were offered outrageously low—indeed, criminal —prices, we donated to our neighborhood public library. It was a matter of principle.

On the particular day of my Discovery, I had sneaked a *Dime Mystery* from off a candy store newsstand, slipped it under my coat, held it fast with my pocketed hand, and began my "casual," always thrilling, walking getaway. Almost immediately, however, a strong hand collared me. It was the owner's son, "an older guy," likely eighteen or so years old.

"I'm taking you home. Right now. March." And, just like that, my sudden destination was disaster. My parents were entertaining company in the flat, and images of my father's shame and then anger, as I, Gangster, was hauled before them, consumed me in dread.

I tried reasoning with my captor. I made light, ha ha, sure I was going to pay you. I wheedled. I negotiated. In return for my release, I offered to work all day sweeping the candy store, polishing, *anything*, "for free," for two days, for a *week*! It was to no avail. Finally, as we were approaching our tenement house, I played my trump card. I had been holding it in reserve, planning its play as a last resort. My clincher, my ultimate deal in exchange for my freedom, was to give him all the money that I had. I proffered, certain it could not be refused, my week's allowance, my nickel.

He refused it.

I was stunned. A nickel! Refused . . .

Such resolute principle had to be admired. Grudgingly, somewhat awed, I did.

Father and Son, Man and Boy

Cockeye Georgie and I sneak into Madison Square Garden. The smile and the arm wave you saw in the rotogravure section of the Sunday News. I feel superior to adults. A quarter of a century later. So dazzling, even beautiful was his footwork. Once again.

In 1936 when I was thirteen, and Franklin Delano Roosevelt was campaigning in New York City for reelection to the Presidency, Cockeye Georgie and I sneaked into Madison Square Garden to hear him speak. More accurately, we snuck into the Garden, Because It Was There, and the New York Paramount, the Roxy and several lesser scaling peaks were no longer the challenges they had been when we were young, like twelve. Of course, the fact that the President of the United States was appearing, added to our sense of derring-do.

More exhilaration when we found two seats together. Our problem—we did have one, such as it was—was to contain our self satisfaction; it fairly effervesced in us. It wasn't so much that we were in the presence of the President—remember, this was 1936, Before TV, when Presidents were as remote as kings—or that we were participating in an Historical Event, but that for all the omnipresent police, for all that thousands of adults were milling about Eighth Avenue, unable to gain lawful entry, slippery we were In. The contemplation of it all pleasured our larcenous hearts.

When Roosevelt appeared, the smile and the arm wave you saw in the rotogravure section of the *Sunday News*, the audience rose as one, and rising, roared its affection. After a few moments Georgie and I sat down. Not so the crowd. It remained up, roaring its twenty thousand voiced welcome, climbing atop its seats to better see Him. We were awed, and a little frightened too. All those adults, all those flush faced, by now hoarsely shouting people, some, hands cupping mouths, some, arms flailing and fists stabbing the air, some climbing atop their seats, each oblivious to the other, all, body and soul, focused on the smiling face hung in the spotlight. At one point either Georgie said to me or I to him, one of us said it, I don't remember which, They've been cheering for *ten* minutes! And then, while I was experiencing both the wonder and the fear of it all, why I am writing this began to happen. Suddenly, Georgie, my every-mood companion, was no longer sitting, was himself up, standing tip toe on his seat, shouting crazily, his face a stranger's. I remember thinking that now I know what "mob psychology" means and I felt superior to all these adults, they seemed no more than a multithroated Animal, and I felt disappointment too, in Georgie, he had succumbed and while thinking these thoughts, it all climaxed—indelibly. Suddenly, yet it seemed gradually, I became aware of my own straining throat muscles, heard my own shouting voice, *already hoarse,* became aware that I was jumping up and down, atop my seat. With the insight you sometimes have when drunk, I realized—without recalling a single step in my flash transformation—that I had become one with the Animal.

A quarter of a century later, my companion now my ten year old son, I paid our way into the Miami Beach Auditorium and remembered Franklin Delano Roosevelt, Georgie, and myself because much the same thing happened. My boy had been enthralled by TV boxing and wrestling matches and so I thought I'd take him to the fights where he could see the sordidness of the real thing, and so get boxing out of his system. My plan was working well. The preliminaries featured unevenly matched fighters and the resultant brutality evoked the crowd's sadistic response. Great. Just what I wanted to happen. Now Deanie would get his fill of boxing for life and turn his interests to baseball or space or whatever. But my hopes were short-lived. The top of the card featured a then little known boxer with the unlikely name, Cassius Clay. So dazzling, even beautiful, was his footwork, so much like a finely tooled, so-fast-it-was-almost-invisible piston rod, did his left move, that in no time I was cheering him on, my rhetoric on the brutality of boxing forgotten—by both of us. Once again, I had become one with the mob.

When China-watchers wonder at the marauding Red Guard being but a single generation removed from the tradition of Chinese ancestor respect, accumulated over millenia, and at the single generation that separates their radical guerrilla youth from its liberal parents, I don't share their puzzling wonder. A generation isn't all that short a time for rational man to revert to mob man. Man and boy, it's taken me seconds.

Hello Harry

When I die. Either God or English grammar. Why he cried. Hello Harry.

I have asked that when I die, I be buried in Miami. Miami, because of its sunshine, its far skies and Dufy waters, or as I like to put it, because you can breathe there. I gave up a long held preference to be cremated when a dear friend was. Upon seeing the urn containing his ashes, I thought, Add water and instant Morris! That did it. Besides, a burial plot gives the children a place to intend visiting, someday.

New England country cemeteries are charming, and especially so the historic one in Concord, Massachusetts. I think of it however as a nice place to visit, but as a Jew, I wouldn't want to live there.

The cemeteries in New York City and environs depress me. It's as if New York City, strangler of life, relentlessly pursued its prey, even into death. I mean the tombstones packed as tight as subway straphangers, the rumbling street and the roaring sky noises that reverberate through those Queens cemeteries, the foul city air that spills into them. In New York, even in death, no way out.

All this is *apropos* my having attended the burial of my father-in-law. He died at seventy-two and if he had been "important" enough to warrant a newspaper obituary, it would have said that death came "after a long illness." And it was long. For all the nearly thirty years that I knew him, he suffered from a faltering heart. Also, the last fifteen years of his life were spent in total blindness. Still, in all of the years that I knew him, I do not recall a single time that he complained. Tears sometimes formed in those eye sockets, but he never voiced them. His days and his nights, for hours and hours without end, were spent with his braille books. The books never varied in all the years that he endlessly fingered them. One was a Hebrew language bible, the other a massive tome on English grammar. It seemed as if he could never know quite well enough, either God or English grammar.

But to return to his health and what I want to tell about him. Whenever I thought of him, the image that formed in my mind was that of an invalid. A sweet man, a good man, but everlastingly an invalid. It was most everybody's image. Maybe he knew this; maybe that's why he cried. I think so because hours before he died, the coma in which he had been sinking parted somewhat, let through several moments of surfacing consciousness. He recognized his son and to the younger man's intently posed attention, said, as if explaining himself, "I was so nice looking, so strong."

His burial plot is one of several that were purchased many years ago by the *landsmen* of the City of Deveen of pre-World War I Russia. Most of the *landsmen* who are buried there knew him as a young man when he was nice looking and strong. Standing there, thinking sad thoughts of him, I thought a glad one too. Wouldn't it be right if these Deveeners he was rejoining, recognized him just as he remembered himself? No hesitation, no trying to place his expression faintly recognizable behind the death mask he had been so long breaking in, but recognized him right away, Hello Harry. He would like that. For all that this subway cemetery was nothing more than a change of slum address venue, he would like that.

NAZIS AND JEWS
AND BYGONES REVISITED

Before I begin what I want to say, I want to say something.

In 1963, eighteen years after Hitler, when I was already forty years old, I visited Germany as a member of an Anti-Defamation League of B'nai B'rith mission, invited by the Federal Republic to come and see the goodness of their intentions. For a month I stayed and I saw, and when I came home I published my diary notes. Previously, I had never kept a diary. Even as a boy, first-time experiencing love and hate, joy and sorrow, certain that never before had these emotions been realized quite as richly, I hadn't felt the need to diary cage them. In Germany, however, long since no longer a boy, more numbed than feeling, more drained than full, I needed desperately my note book, needed to talk to it so that nightly I might experience in delayed reaction, the scenes I shadow moved through by day.

When I returned to the States, my notes were published by a small magazine concerned with Jewish affairs. Oddly, one brief entry was dropped by the editor. Likely he was guided by dictates of taste. That entry, however, more so than all of the others, contained the spur for my compulsion, The War long over, myself now middle-aged, to write of Nazis and Jews. This was the entry.

Nazis and Jews
and Bygones Revisited

Jews and Nazis share something in common that is so totally, so exclusively their own, so intimately theirs and theirs alone, that no one, absolutely no one, can fully understand it. The Nazi sympathizer wasn't so close to the Nazi, the Christian martyr dying protecting Jews wasn't so close to Jews, as the Nazi and the Jew are close to each other. Theirs, only theirs, is the oneness, the hysterical oneness of that frozen moment when the wide, wild eyes of the rapist and the wide, wild eyes of the raped lock, when the defiler helplessly defiles and the defiled is haplessly defiled.

The moment frozen, endlessly they shame and pain and die in their endless nightmare, the Germans and the Jews, in their endlessly anguished Togetherness.

The diary notes follow.

THESE PINK AND BLONDE WOMEN

Bad Godesberg: Weird, me being here. I almost wrote, me, Jew, being here. When's the last time I felt so consciously Jewish? Or, for that matter, so consciously American? The nearest I've come to Germany is Coney Island, or maybe the Statue of Liberty is nearer, and yet I'm bugged by the feeling that I've been here before. It's as if I've walked through Bad Godesberg before, albeit I don't remember thinking it charming. I've seen before, I think I've seen before, these pink and blonde women, these fat but stolid men and the long-striding, so healthy, teenagers. Was it way back in Brooklyn, and fully twenty-five years ago? Probably, Fox Movietone News. Sad and resonant voiced Lowell Thomas, and on the screen, kneeling, bearded, Jews and pink and fat Germans jeering; and the theatre in our Jewish neighborhood as utterly and hysterically silent as the nightmare of a deaf mute. And now I'm here, here in Germany, and of course I have been here before. It was the sunlight that confused me, the surprise of the sunlight after leaving that movie, and shining on these clean people and their charming homes, that's what confused me.

HITLER'S FAVORITE HOTEL

Bad Godesberg: Ironic, that we should be staying at the Dreesen Hotel. In this hotel, in the very meeting room in which we met yesterday afternoon, Hitler and Chamberlain worked out the Munich Pact. Hitler's favorite hotel, they say. There's a George Washington Slept Here gag somewhere in that. Still, I slept like a log last night, my first night here, and for all I know on Adolf's own pad, and that's interesting too, my sleeping so peacefully; here, I mean.

A JURY OF PEERS

Bonn: I liked the men in the Ministry of Justice. Young, straight, knowledgeable. Harry asked them to comment on the very low ratio of prosecutions of Nazis to crimes committed by them. Something like 5,000 prosecutions for millions of murders, untold plunder, etc. Also, we wanted to know how come convicted murderers, involving multiple killings, have been getting paltry four year sentences. Answers: The Nuremberg Trials revealed that Nazis were rarely personally involved in the execution of crimes. Local help, Poles for instance, were willing and efficient accomplices. The Federal Republic is without jurisdiction in these cases. Also, numbers of murderers fled; numbers were tried in foreign courts; an indeterminate number were killed in the course of the war. Finally, natural death—it's almost twenty years since Germany's surrender—has thinned the line-up.

Another lawyer took the ball at this point. He told of prosecuting a case in 1950 in which the defendants were charged with the Crystal Night pogrom of 1938. Twelve years had elapsed, and the state's witnesses were hazy, uncertain, self-contradictory. He lost the case. Still, he says, if you believe in the democratic principle that every man is entitled to his day in court, and to a trial before a jury of his peers, this is it. I had half the feeling when he referred to peers and local juries that he was thinking of ours in Alabama, Mississippi, and what the hell do we do about it? Dispose of trial by jury? Like Hitler? As to the light sentences returned by local juries, he reminded us that the top Nazis were tried and convicted by Allied courts. Today, they're free. Who freed them? The Allies. His point: that if local juries are aware, and they are aware, that the Allies have commuted the sentences of the big Nazis, should we, they reason, pass harsher sentences on the small fry who simply followed the big shots' orders? I didn't argue.

WERE THE DAHLIAS SO RED?

Frankfurt: This country is beautiful. God, it's beautiful. And the flowers, their rich profusion of color, and the morning mist on the Rhine, like a Japanese print. The women, early morning walking to the grocer's, and the kids, they do have square heads, all so much like a color picture in the *National Geographic Magazine*. Were the dahlias so red, was the morning grass so sweet, the children so cherub fresh then too? Somehow they shouldn't have been, but they were and you keep wondering, with all this beauty around them, how could they have been so unspeakably evil?

"I HAVE BEEN AWAY FOR 1,000 YEARS"

Frankfurt: Professor R was at a disadvantage with us. A good man, a bright man, he looked and sounded so much like a vaudeville caricature of a giddy German professor it distracted us. Until he got down to business.

Referring to his having been a refugee from Nazism's vaunted Thousand Year Reich, he referred to his twelve year exile with: "I have been away for 1,000 years." We started paying attention.

A sociologist, he observed that the new generation is isolated from its elders in Germany as nowhere else. The kids learn about the Nazi Reich in school, or in paperbacks, or on TV, and when they come and ask questions— what were you doing then, Dad?—they get evasions, irritations, or lame rationalizations. And so the gulf between the generations. The professor feels that the rejection by the young of the old, the "isolation" from home in which the young are developing, is "admirable."

All over the United States, and the world I suppose, viewers with alarm deplore the new generation and its straying from parental standards and values. Here, it's "admirable." What a comment, what a judgment—and by what judges!—on the entire generation of Hitler *heilers*; to be sentenced to the rejection, even loathing, at best quiet hostility, of your own children. By comparison the Nuremberg sentences are overtime parking tickets.

A TALE OF TWO CEMETERIES

Frankfurt: Visited two Jewish cemeteries in Frankfurt today. In the first we came across a section with hundreds of tombstones, all alike, all telling the same story. So and so, age such and such, died January, 1942. So and so, such and such age, died March, 1942. In all, some 750 markers, each one with an early 1942 date. Turns out that all of them were suicides, all of them. Killed themselves when they received deportation orders to the concentration camps. Seven hundred and fifty persons, teenagers, mamas and papas, whole families, widows, widowers, a community by God, in a macabre mass charade of "escape." Hurree! Hurree! Hurree! See It Live, Right Before Your Veree Eyes! Cast of Hundreds! 750, Yes, 750 Real Live Acts. Seven fucking hundred and fifty souls, each poor bastard killing himself, herself, the children, rather than face the Nazi tomorrow. Poor bastards, poor, poor souls...

And the other cemetery. It has a wall on which is listed Frankfurt's Jewish soldiers who died in action in World War I. After each of their names is "Died for the Fatherland."

GERMAN JEWS OR JEWS IN GERMANY?

Frankfurt: Before going to the cemeteries we visited with a number of Frankfurt Jews. Subject of their discussion:

Are we German Jews or are we Jews in Germany? Twenty years later and they're still wrangling about their identity. Had the issue been put to a vote, the Jews-in-Germany side would have won. I'd have voted with them, then. But they're wrong. Germany is their home by choice. To stay on and feel this alienation is masochistic. The we're-German-Jews group is affirming life as something more than a private pain. They're healthier. Still, I feel closer to the others. Emotionally, anyway.

HITLER'S KEPT PROMISE

Cologne: These Jews here, they're remnants. Old, gnarled and scarred ruins. They are long ago yesterdays and looking at them there's only the faintest flickering suggestion that they may have a tomorrow. No young ones and damn few who are even fortyish. Ironic, for all of the well intended philo-Semitism of the Bonn Government, there simply aren't any Jews here to be philo to. A *Judenrein* Germany, Hitler's one ultimately successful campaign?

THE STATE DINNER

Cologne: Now, before I go to sleep, I'd best get this down. The dinner tonight, I suppose it was a "state dinner," was an extraordinary experience. Tomorrow, maybe I'll write about the German as host, of the way in which the trout was served, like it was live, of the wines, etc. But now while it's with me, about the dinner.

Ten of them; ten of us. Ten German officials, some ex-Nazis, and ten Jews whose profession is combatting anti-Semitism. The meal and its breaking of bread, the sitting down to it and the small-talk comraderie all symbolized a kind of blood-brother ceremony. All of us were conscious of it. I think too that when the meal was over there was general disinclination to follow the unwritten but unyielding script that calls for "remarks." But what else can you do, play poker?

Ben's remarks, three minutes worth, had the right touch—brief, casually dignified. Herr A's response was in kind. It should have been left there. It wasn't. Two of ours, like it was a Quaker meeting, felt the need to rise and also make remarks. They spoke eloquently, even movingly about the warm spirit of the dinner, the threshold that it was to a new relationship between Germans and Jews. One of them recreated his personal and his family's suffering during the Hitler years and, obviously deeply moved by the evening, his voice faltering with emotion, he toasted the new German-Jewish brotherhood. Many of the men, theirs and ours, were reached—deep down. I wasn't. I wished I could get the hell out of there.

Here's why. It's like when a man and a woman have a violent, soul searing and gut goring battle. They hate each other, can kill each other. That night, in bed, in the crazy chemistry of mind and body, they turn to each other and wordlessly know each other. What wanted saying is said, said clearly in that silent, remorseful, mutually aggressing, ravenous embrace. No talk. Maybe later, they light a cigarette.

Our eating and drinking together tonight, we Jews and ex-Nazis, was a deep intimacy. Talking the talk of haters and lovers was too much. We should have simply lit cigarettes.

HOME IS WHERE THEY SERVE CHOW MEIN

Cologne: Six weeks overseas and I'm starved for an American meal. This evening we prowled the main drag in Cologne looking for a hamburger joint. No luck. Finally we saw a neon sign beckoning us to what, after all, is our native dish. A Chinese restaurant. I was home again.

I VINDICATE EISENHOWER

Cologne: I'm a fool for having felt that way, but I'm still enjoying it. We moved in to Count N's home today. We'll stay a week to get the feel of the "grass roots," how the man in the street lives, and so on. (A Count? The Man In The Street?) The Count greeted us in the garden and in the groping small talk of host-for-a-week and total strangers, asked me if I shoot. I said ye-es, but it's been almost twenty years. In less time than it takes to say Fritz Mueller he's in and out of the house, offers me a rifle and points to a sparrow on a nearby tree, inviting me to kill it. I react—I was so startled—like a boy scout, asking why on earth, etc. The Count explains that he loves birds, has feeders for them in the garden and that the sparrows chase away the singing birds. *Ergo*, the sparrows must go. By this time, thank goodness, the sparrow's elsewhere and out of sight. Now, the Count invites me to shoot an apple off a tree and I set myself in position, squeeze the trigger and bring new hope to the breasts of neighborhood sparrowlife. I missed—ignominiously. Next, the Count. He takes the rifle, no fooling, no posing, simply lifts it and bang, the apple is cut in half. This, I see, is a host whom I'm going to have to try to like.

Later in the afternoon, the Count and his twelve year old daughter invite me to a game of croquet. I've never played it, but it looks like fun. The Count wins, I barely beat the child, and I'm wondering if maybe these people aren't, in fact, a superior race. By this time, the seven year old boy wants in, and now the four of us are malleting the ball across the lawn. And wouldn't you know, the three of them, father, daughter, and son, lead me through the last wicket! There's laughter, kidding, and I, stiff-upper-lipped, make with ha-ha too. Tea follows and while they're drinking tea and making conversation with Abe, I casually pick up a mallet and take a few practice swings, using the golf stance rather than the swing-it-between-the legs stance. A few practice swings, and I'm ready for bear. "How 'bout it, Count," I nonchalantly, so very nonchalantly, sing out, "want to give it another go?" The kids whoop yes, the Count smiles okay—I suppose it really wasn't patronizing—and I'm invited to lead off.

Man, did I clobber them! I went through the wickets in record time, and, simultaneously, must have set a record for minimum swings!

Silly? I suppose. But it felt so good, like the U.S. really did win the war, like I really was in the Marines. That apple, those first two games, I felt as if Eisenhower, Normandy, Patton, all were lies. Now, the American soldier, Jewry, the Allies were vindicated! I still feel good about it.

A TYPICAL GERMAN HOME

Cologne: Father von G is nice. Looks like Fernandel. On the way to his mother's home he reminded us that she's a war widow. "You might not consider a widow's home as a typical German home, but it is. We lost fifteen million men in the war." His being a nice guy, he saying it, I felt saddened.

His mother's home is interesting. In the living room, a picture of her late husband, a uniformed three star general in Hitler's army. Beside him is his father, the priest's paternal grandfather, also in uniform, and he was a four star general in the Kaiser's army. Daddy is a Hollywood type caster's cliché for the Nazi general and granddaddy, same, for the stiffnecked Junker general.

Father von G's kid brother is studying in England and I got a kick out of his room. Picasso prints, Chagall (!) prints, college-age bric-a-brac, pipes. Could've been my own college room.

I liked Mrs. von G. Mothery, dignified, intelligent. No patronizing airs. Didn't even mention that her husband had been part of the 20th of July plot on Hitler's life. (Father von G also didn't mention it.)

Still, it's all very confusing. If she were not nice, if she were haughty, if she were stiff or proud, she'd fit snugly into the casting office's file on the wives of Nazi big shots. But she's nice and that's what's so confusing. Was her husband, the three star general, also nice? I gather he was. The priest is nice, the general was nice, momma is nice. Were they all "nice people?" Has it any real meaning, being nice?

LINDY'S IN COLOGNE

Cologne: The waiters here in Cologne seem to have taken a correspondence course from Lindy's. The Count, fearing we'll be late for the theater, asks one of them if he can pay the bill, and the guy answers, "I hope so." I get a five mark note in change, ask the waiter who the girl pictured on the mark is, and he says, "Can't tell you. You don't seem the type to keep a secret!" They recommend "Cologne caviar" and it's blutwurst; they recommend "half a chicken" and it's a roll and cheese.

GERMANS AND ENGLISHMEN

Cologne: Several Germans have remarked to me that they don't like the English. I asked one why, and he said, "They're arrogant." *Gott in himmel!*

THE SCHOOL KIDS, THE PRINCIPAL, THE COUNT

Cologne: Liking, or trying to like "good Germans" is like trying to love a reformed prostitute. She's being a lady, she's trying hard, you begin to forget her past and then boom, unwittingly, unconsciously, she says or does something that reminds you of what she was, of what she can be again.

I've been to several schools in the past few days. The kids are good kids. Whether it be in the schools, on TV, in paperbacks, or wherever, they are getting "good" values. And these values are offered up by "good Germans." But then the slip shows and you wonder.

In one classroom the kids had been learning about Bismarck. They were taught how he unified Germany and made it an important power through "Blood and Iron." We engaged the students in discussion, querying them as to their views of the same "Blood and Iron" policy as a means of reunifying today's split Germany. Without exception they responded that while the great hero's method worked in the 19th Century it wouldn't do today. Today we must talk. War is no solution. Use the United Nations. It was all very encouraging.

In another classroom, twelve year olds, we asked the children what they knew of the Hitler years. Students aren't taught about Hitler until they're fourteen. We were curious as to what they had absorbed outside the classroom. One told of the "great congresses" that were held then; another knew that Hitler built the expressways; another commented that while everybody hates Hitler now, then they all loved him; still another volunteered that everyone was employed; he was followed by a kid who offered the information that women had to work. We prompted them further, asking whether they had any information concerning the Third Reich and Jews. One poor kid told how his mother had to run all over Germany, chased apparently, because "they" mistakenly thought she was Jewish; another child referred to "showers" and their use as a means of killing Jews; another thought that Jewish stars were burned into the arms of Jews; another had heard that Jews were spat upon. There was no nostalgia for the Third Reich, no childish romanticism about marching and might, but rather a sober, kind of frightened, recalling of things they had heard.

In each and every classroom, and we've visited some half dozen, the kids queried us about Alabama and Mississippi. Not the hostile, "if you're such a great democracy, how about . . ." questions. On the contrary, they were groping questions by sincerely confused children, children who have been taught that democracy is an ideal form of government and that its natural habitat is in the United States. Why then the Negro sit-ins, the Negro marches, the unsolved bombings of Negro churches, homes? It was almost as if they wanted assurances from us that it wasn't so or if so, that there was some simple, as yet undiscovered by them, explanation, one that didn't soil the democratic ideal. I felt sorry for them, for their disillusion. But to return to my opening thought about "good Germans."

Following a really rewarding experience in a classroom, we accompanied the principal back to his office. He
sensed that his visiting firemen were pleased with what he
had shown them. He relaxed. So much so, we soon got into
a bull session. Naturally enough, the conversation went
back to the Hitler years, and damned if he didn't confide
in us that anti-Semitism wouldn't have been so successful
had not the Eastern European Jews monopolized the important posts in the professions!

All right, so he's sixty and he hasn't been purged of
all his anti-Semitic notions. It shouldn't surprise. The important thing is that he's teaching kids and doing a good
job of it. Still, his ignorance of the dynamics of bigotry
aside, I felt that his facts were wrong. That night, seeking
to confirm my own recollection of Germany in the Thirties, I asked the Count whether it was his impression that
there were significant numbers of Eastern European Jews
in Germany during the days of the Weimar Republic. No,
he says, and asks why I asked. Feeling close to him and
genuinely friendly after several days of living together, I
tell him about my conversation with the principal. When
I'm through, the Count shakes his head and mutters
Dummy, a real Dummy, that principal. It couldn't have
been the reason for the success of anti-Semitism because
there simply weren't any Eastern European Jews to talk
of here. The reason for Hitler's successful program against
Jews was that the important posts were held by *German*
Jews and they "demonstrated their success too much."
Not wanting to sprawl over a language barrier, I inquired,
"Demonstrated?" "You know," says he, "they showed off
too much."

The principal is a force for good in Germany. No
question about it. But the old poison still lingers. It's dormant, but there. The Count is one of democracy's best

friends in Germany, and as reliable a sympatico friend of the Jews as one might hope to find here. He's thirty-seven, too young to know who was or wasn't Jewish in the Weimar days, but in him too, the Goebbels fantasy lingers. These are the "good Germans," and they are.

HOPALONG HANS CASSIDY

Cologne: Anticipating all kinds of earth shaking implications in their answers, we asked a classroom of fourteen year olds who they most want to be like when they grow up. And so who are German youths' heroes? Jerry Lewis, Rock Hudson, Benny Goodman. The one German mentioned is a long dead author who wrote cowboy stories!

PROVING A NEGATIVE

Cologne: Talk of catharsis! The dinner party was going along pleasantly enough, and that's just what prompted me to say what I did. I mean, all the small talk and each of us being charmingly clever like it was any one of fifty thousand Saturday night suburban parties back home. Over and over again, I had the feeling, What the hell am I doing here? And so I told the Count and the Countess, Herr F and his wife, that I had a confession to make. I told them about my afternoon walk with Father von G through the town cemetery; how we paused before a stone that read, "Hans Schmidt, 18 years old, Stalingrad"; how, notwithstanding the boy's age, I felt no pity, but instead, not without bitterness, I found myself thinking, Who invited him there?

I continued, telling them of Father von G's comment while I was thinking my private thoughts; that he knew the family and that they were "fine people." Knowing the priest well by now and liking him, I knew that his estimate, "fine people," was one, had I known them, I'd likely have shared. His words dissipated my indifference to the dead boy, but not my bitterness for Stalingrad. I grew vaguely troubled and that I still was, was my confession.

I suppose the deeply personal nature of my remarks, the cognac—to be sure, the cognac—changed the tone of the party. The Count revealed that he had been "an enthusiastic Hitler youth leader" and Herr F, withered arm though he has, offered that he had been a Hitler youth leader too, and later, a member of the Party.

Somehow I wasn't surprised by the Count's having been "an enthusiastic" young Nazi. He shoots enthusiastically, plays croquet enthusiastically, and dammit if he isn't an enthusiastic liberal! What's more, I'm sure that he enthusiastically cultivates Jewish friends. I suspect that there's more than one enthusiastic ex-Nazi who today is an enthusiastic good-guy while the indifferent to Nazism guy, as a consequence of his personality type, is today indifferent about German democracy.

But I wanted to write down Herr F's remarks. During the Thirties his closest friend, in appearance more Aryan than he, was Jewish. "I knew, we all knew, Hitler's views on Jews, but we told ourselves that nothing would happen to the Jews we knew. After all, we told ourselves, our Jewish friends were not the kind that Hitler was talking about. At the end of the war, I went home to the Sudetenland to look for my friend, and as if to confirm what subconsciously I knew all along, but which I refused to think about, I went directly from the train to the Jewish cemetery." Was it sentimental slobbery? The cognac? Gutrooted sincerity? His voice choked as he whispered, "I found him there."

We asked him what made him a Nazi. His answer: idealism. Hitler's platform, cleanliness of mind and body, honesty in government, purging the nation of social and political decadence. "About Jews," he continued, "we have a faculty—man, that is—to block out on things we don't want to believe. And when in the closing years of the war rumors reached us about the extermination camps, rumors we had every reason to believe, we still would not see. By now we had our own families to think about, virtually every German family suffered losses, our own lives to somehow salvage in the bombing wreckage, and so we continued to block out on the genocide in our midst."

And how did you become an ex-Nazi?

"In the late Forties I was applying for a visa to the United States where an international conference to which I was a delegate was being held. An American sergeant, the bureaucrat in charge, routinely asked me if I had ever been a Nazi. I don't know what prompted me to tell the truth. It would have been so easy to simply say no. But I said yes. The sergeant's cigar almost dropped out of his mouth. When he recovered from my answer, he asked me if I was still a Nazi. I mumbled no, I wasn't. He said, prove it. And now I was speechless. How does one prove a negative? Proof that I was a Nazi was simple: that I wasn't a Nazi, impossible. But at that point, an inspiration hit me. I held up this useless, deformed arm. I said to him, when I was young I had polio. I can't have it again. He gave me the visa."

All of this, quietly, so quietly we could hear each other's breath.

The Count again. We asked him—and Herr F too—about their "idealism" in 1938. After all, the German

press was full of the pictures of Crystal Night, of the violence and the humiliation visited upon Jews. What of the
intellectual Nazi's idealism then, and where was the good
German's reaction?

The hour was late already, the cognac and the naked
conversation softened and hushed the room, and in a kind
of oral slow motion the Count whispered, "We were cow-
ards."

THE WHITE HORSE AND THE 20th OF JULY

Berlin: Two unrelated items and my single, related reaction.

In Bonn, Cologne and Frankfurt when we were there,
and now in Berlin, people have told us of the *Weisse
P ferde*—the White Horse—the nickname for Ferdinand
Weiss, a famous and apparently beloved German comedian in the time of the Third Reich. Virtually alone, he had
the temerity to ridicule Hitler. He paid for it with several
short prison terms. In recalling him, each of the people
retold some of his gags—each one telling the identical
stories.

Weiss would come out on stage at The Porcupine, a
political cabaret in Berlin, and hurl his arm out in what
seemed like the Nazi salute. Holding it in position for a
moment, he'd lower it slightly, turn his palm over, arm
still extended, and finally observe, "No, it's not raining."
Or, he'd come marching out to the center of the stage,
click his heels, make the Nazi salute, and intone, "Heil—
heil—er, er, what's his name again?" The *Weisse P ferde*
story that is consistently told with the most relish is how
he came out on stage, laboriously pushing a large wooden
crate. After getting it front and center with amusing

pantomime, he'd open the box and pull out three large framed pictures: Hitler, Goering, Goebbels. Propping the pictures up against the crate so that the audience could view them, he'd walk back and forth pretending perplexed concentration and finally—his pantomime and his fame for double entendre having brought the audience to a heightened expectation—he would turn to the audience and muse: "Tell me, shall I put them up against the wall, or simply hang them."

Now, the unrelated, second item.

Today we visited the 20th of July Memorial. That's the memorial to the men who in 1944 tried unsuccessfully to assassinate Hitler in the famous bomb plot. The government has been attempting to make the 20th of July a national holiday and in army education courses the leaders of the 20th of July are offered up as heroes who gave their lives for the honor of Germany. The memorial itself is the prison to which the leading plotters were hustled off and hung on meat hooks. The huge cell in which they were murdered—Hitler had movies taken of the butchery so that he might later enjoy it—has been left much as it was. It's dark; it's foreboding; it's a moving shrine to brave men.

But my joint reaction to the *Weisse P ferde* and the 20th of July. Everywhere in Germany the same anti-Hitler jokes of the White Horse are told and retold to me. It was funny the first time and even the second time, but after a while I had the feeling that the retelling of these same stories—twenty years later—was a kind of political aside whispered in my ear, assuring me, "See, we didn't slavishly follow Hitler. Nosirree, bub! We, in our own way, fought back!"

And the 20th of July movement. I remember their "conditions" for peace with the Allies. Germany to retain the booty Hitler had won prior to England's entry into the war!

These then are the symbols of Third Reich anti-Nazi heroism. A brave and principled night club comic and a movement of Hamlets (1944!) that mustered its bravery after Crystal Night, after the Anschluss, after Czechoslovakia, after Poland, after Rotterdam, after the camps, after the war was all but over.

These are Heroes. German Democratic Heroes. Color them Grey.

NEW YEAR'S DAY IN BERGEN BELSEN

Berlin: I suppose as good a way as any to describe the Open Door is to call it a Salvation Army serving the emotional needs of people. Really, it's more. Jesuit sponsored, it's situated in downtown Berlin on a street between the business section and a street of garish joints. People with domestic problems, personal problems, or any kind of emotional dislocation can come in and talk things over with a trained psychologist. Picked up some interesting miscellaneous information. For instance, that here in West Berlin, as thriving a city as there is in Europe, there is also Europe's highest suicide rate. Pathetically, the rate rose even higher with the building of the Wall. Interesting, too, is the fact that considerable numbers of colored people visit the Open Door. Why do they come? Usually out of frustration resulting from an inability to rent an apartment! There are some 40,000 mulattoes in West Germany, souvenirs left behind by our Armed Forces.

Frau T, the psychologist in charge, told of the sharp increase in the numbers of people with torturous guilt feelings who have been seeking help from the Open Door since the showing of *The Deputy*. That's the play by Rolf

Hochhuth that's attracting so much attention, that is un-reservedly critical of Pope Pius XII for his alleged indif-ference to the Nazi genocide of Jews. I asked her, "Are they former SS men, or concentration camp guards that are coming in?"

"Oh no," she responded. "Young people are coming in. People who were obviously children during the Hitler years. They are the ones burdened with guilt. The older people do not come. They have made an accommodation with their past."

Yes and no, I suppose. When we visited the Bergen Belsen Concentration Camp a couple of weeks ago, I saw something that disposes me toward a less resigned viewpoint. Here's a camp that's remote from any main highway, that offers absolutely no comforts—I don't re-member seeing even a bench—that is simply a stark, ex-cruciating reminder of the Nazi terror and terrorists. We were there on a weekday; it was *Rosh Hashonah*; we came to pray for the dead. And notwithstanding its distance from any city, its unrelieved poignancy, it having been the middle of the week, there were scores of young people there. Young people soberly, somberly walking among the monuments, thinking God knows what kind of sad, sad thoughts, making God knows what kind of vows. And there were older Germans there too. Doing the same thing. No, not all have made an accommodation. Some remem-ber and can't forget and are teaching their young. Not much more can be asked of them.

THE WALL, THEIRS AND MINE

Berlin: Visited East Berlin today. A public confessional. There are the beautiful streets, the buildings, the monu-ments, but something there is about them that is—well, frightening. It's like a Dali painting. The subject matter is there, almost normal, but you look again and it's limp, empty, eerie. Tree-lined streets, attractive shops, handsome buildings, but all of them empty, all limply suspended in a twilight zone, sadly silent, immobile, like a Dali canvas.

Returning to West Berlin, we drove along the Wall. Our newspapers and our TV never fully communicated to me the utter evil, the overwhelming sadness of the Wall. Miles of ugly brick, capped by jagged pieces of glass stuck into the top layer of cement, and over the glass, ominous barbed wire. On the east side, deserted streets, here and there a rifleman, and the feeling that in those buildings, behind the blinds, people are peering over the wall, hoping to catch a glimpse of freedom. On the west side, memorial markers to Herr so-and-so or Frau so-and-so who jumped to freedom and landed in death. West Berliners standing in line to climb a platform from which to look over the wall and perhaps catch a glimpse of a mother, a father, a friend. Depressing. So depressing.

But like so much that I have experienced here, for me the Wall too has reverse English.

This evening we had dinner with Herr B. After dinner, he showed movie slides. The first slide was of the Brandenberg Gate and seeing it again, all of the morning's sadness returned to me. Sadness for these people whose city, families and circles of friends have been sundered by Communist evil. Then came the second slide. Again the Brandenberg Gate, but this time all lit up, its statuary glowing warmly and happily, and you couldn't but feel warm and happy too at this graphic representation of Before Communism.

Not for long, however. For through the darkened room came Herr B's voice and his running commentary. "I took this picture in the good old days. 1936."

Of course, he meant nothing. Like the principal, like the Count, he's a good man and I genuinely like him. But, 1936, the good old days? For the moment there in the dark, I wished the Wall long life and to hell with them all. It's hard, so hard, to be purely rational about these people. Maybe our kids will be able to manage it; I can't.

EPILOGUE

And so these reflections on my boyhood and on my middle years, these introspections on my *Yiddishe neshuma* and about my political bones, end with what? With Nazism recalled. It's fitting. We grew up together, the Nazis and my generation of Jewish liberals. As our contemporary, Hitler taught us better than did Hebrew School that we were Jews and that no matter the Rothschilds, the Einsteins, the Hank Greenbergs, being Jewish was a hazardous condition. And though Nazism and our youth both happened a long time ago, and now are both long gone, I remain their remembering child. So it is that the grown man of me probes even issues innocent of religious identification, say, Vietnam, the Electoral College, German reunification, and you wouldn't guess what miscellaneous else, with, Is It Good For The Jews? This question satisfied, I proceed to the secondary issues, albeit they are primary. For if it's bad for the Jews, my generation still remembers how bad bad can be, and Big Deal troop withdrawal, Big Deal one man one vote, Big Deal the healing of a nation sundered. And if I'm revealing myself to you, I'm also explaining why on so many diverse issues, save a possible Yankees-Mets World Series, rich Jews and poor Jews, educated Jews and not so educated Jews, Northern Jews and Southern Jews, pious Jews and Jews whose religion is irreligion, meld in the phenomenon of a "Jewish position."

And he taught us something else, Hitler. To be sure, the Czars did it for my parents, but Hitler did it for us. He developed our political gutsiness. We are a generation whose politics hang loose, who are wary of white horsed leaders and of concentrated power, no matter its wielders dress in black or in red, their rhetoric elitist or populist. And even if for the moment they are voicing our politics, if they are shouters, we grow suspicious. We have learned and learned dearly that political democracy, for all that it falls short of its declared intentions, for all that it provides refuge for anti-Semites and racists, for all that it is inefficient, insensitive, lumbering, and contradictory, is good for us. Look at us. Look at us in the sciences, in the arts, in government, in the colleges and universities, in our neighborhoods, and see what I mean. To be sure, political democracy may have been too good for us. For as our security as Jews has grown, our identity as Jews has blurred. But alas, that's only continuing proof of the tribulations of being Jewish.

And our children, themselves now young men and women? I have suggested that if they are less Jewish, perhaps it's because we had less affirmative Jewishness to pass on to them, and what we did teach them was diluted with universalism. But the explanation runs deeper than that. Our Judaic classrooms were Dachau and Buchenwald, theirs Scarsdale and Great Neck. How then can they know, really know, about anti-Semitism? Our political professors were Hitler and Stalin, theirs, Kennedy and Johnson and Nixon. So what do they know, really know, about political repression?

But of course, in time, they'll be middle-aged too, and on the one hand that's good, and on the other, it's not so good. It's good because politically and Jewishly, being middle-aged is its own education. It's not so good because poetically, being middle-aged will serve them right.

DATE DUE

6-26			
GAYLORD			PRINTED IN U.S.A.